In the Twilight of Antiquity

The John K. Fesler Memorial Fund
Provided assistance in the publication
of this volume, for which the
University of Minnesota
Press is grateful.

In the Twilight of Antiquity

The R. S. Hoyt Memorial Lectures (1973)

by
Tom B. Jones
Regents' Professor
of History
University of Minnesota

UNIVERSITY OF MINNESOTA PRESS □ MINNEAPOLIS

12-18-78

Preface

These lectures were delivered at the University of Minnesota in the autumn of 1973 as a memorial to that fine scholar, superb teacher, and best of all friends, R. Stuart Hoyt. The proceeds from the series were deposited in a memorial scholarship fund, and such royalties as accrue from the sale of this book will find their way to the same destination.

My choice of subject was dictated by several considerations. Stuart had been the moderator for a fine and well-received series of lectures a decade previously. These were published by the University of Minnesota in 1967. Entitled *Life and Thought in the Early Middle Ages*, they dealt with various aspects of the so-called Dark Ages from the fifth to the eleventh centuries. In view of this and the fact that my remarks must have some relation to the medieval field, it appeared proper and reasonable for me to invade the no-man's-land of the fourth century which Stuart and I had carefully avoided in our long association as colleagues. Why both of us tended to neglect the fourth century, I cannot truly say. But I believe it grew out of some mutual, yet tacit, agreement that our courses should not overlap. Thus, I was accustomed to end Roman History with the retirement of Diocletian in 305, while he, after some preliminary remarks, would begin Medieval History in the fifth century or later.

Nevertheless, even more determinative for me was that many decades previously when I was a student I had read with pleasure—along with the inevitable Gibbon, of course—two works dealing specifically with the fourth century: *Roman Society in the Last Century of the Roman Empire* by Sir Samuel Dill (1898) and *Life and Letters in the Fourth Century* by T. R. Glover (1901). The two were quite different, but each was interesting in its own way, and I never forgot them. The work of Dill, now in paperback, is less acceptable to the young today, or so it seems, and the Glover book has been out of print for a long time. Thus, something a little more contemporary in tone and emphasis seemed to be wanting, but the reader must decide whether I have come near or completely missed the mark.

Therefore, with all due respect for the scholarship of Dill and Glover, for their distinguished successors, and for the serious and important contributions that many young scholars have made to the field, I have ventured to set forth here my own rather untutored impressions of the Later Roman Empire from the days of Constantine to those of Theodosius II.

Tom B. Jones
at Haybank Farm
October 1977

Acknowledgments

First, I am exceedingly grateful to the publishers who have permitted me to reprint translations contained in the following works:

Oxford University Press, H. I. Bell, *The Abinnaeus Archive* (1962); A. Fitzgerald, *The Letters of Synesius of Cyrene* (1926); A. F. Norman, *Libanius, Autobiography* (1965); R. R. Ruether, *Gregory of Nazianzus, Rhetor and Philosopher* (1969).

E. Benn, Ltd., D. Brooke, *Private Letters, Pagan and Christian* (1929).

Society for the Promotion of Christian Knowledge, J. Wilkinson, *Egeria's Travels* (1971).

Princeton University Press, C. Pharr, ed., *The Theodosian Code* (1952).

Harvard University Press (from the Loeb Classical Library), *Ammianus* (3 vols., tr. J. C. Rolfe, 1935-39); *Ausonius* (2 vols., tr. H. G. E. White, 1919-21); St. Basil, the *Letters* (4 vols., tr. R. J. Defarrari, 1926-34); Eunapius, *Lives of the Sophists* (tr. W. C. Wright, 1922); *Greek Anthology* (5 vols. tr. W. R. Paton, 1916-1918); *Works of the Emperor Julian* (3 vols., tr. W. C. Wright, 1913-23).

Second, but by no means least, I wish to express my profound gratitude to good friends who have been helpful in preparing this book for publication: Richard C. Nelson, who drew the maps, and Ernest S. Osgood, for more than two score years my friend and mentor, a great teacher whose careful reading of the manuscript and valuable suggestions demonstrated that he could have been one of the great editors of our time if he had not preferred to devote his life to instructing the young.

TBJ

Table of Contents

Preface v

I. Ferment and Repression 3

II. The Pilgrim 20

III. The Enemy 37

IV. The Orator and the Emperor 52

V. The Churchman 69

VI. The Soldier and the Grammarian 82

VII. The Man of Affairs 96

VIII. The Roman 111

Chronological Summary 128

Imperial Genealogies 130

Notes 133

Select Bibliography 139

Index 145

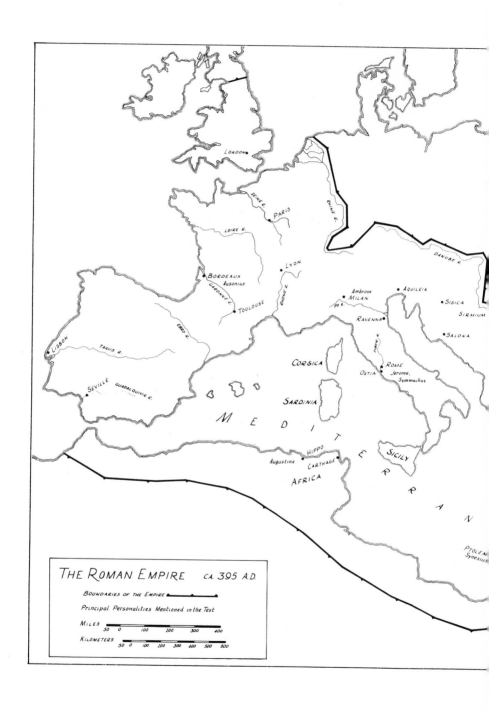

LONDON

SEINE R.

PARIS

RHINE R.

LOIRE R.

DANUBE R.

LYON

BORDEAUX
Ausonius

GARONNE R.

Ambrose
MILAN
PO R.

AQUILEIA

SISICA

TOULOUSE

RHONE R.

SIRMIUM

RAVENNA

SALONA

EBRO R.

LISBON

TAGUS R.

CORSICA

TIBER R.

ROME
Jerome,
Symmachus

OSTIA

SEVILLE GUADALQUIVIR R.

SARDINIA

M E D I T E R R A N

HIPPO

SICILY

Augustine

CARTHAGE

AFRICA

PTOLEN
Synesius

THE ROMAN EMPIRE   CA. 395 A.D.

BOUNDARIES OF THE EMPIRE

Principal Personalities Mentioned in the Text

MILES
50 0   100   200   300   400

KILOMETERS
50 0   100   200   300   400   500   600

SERDICA

ADRIANOPLE
THESSALONICA
CHALCEDON
CONSTANTINOPLE • NIKOMEDIA
NICAEA ANKARA

BLACK SEA

IRIS R.

HALYS R.

PERGAMUM

NYSSA • CAESAREA
NAZIANZUS Cappadocian
Trinity

EPHESUS • TYANA

ATHENS

MAEANDER R.

TARSUS

RHODES

CYPRUS SALAMIS

CRETE

N   SEA

CYRENE

ALEXANDRIA
Palladas
FAYUM
DIONYSIUS
Abinnaeus

NILE R.

SINAI

RED
SEA

ARMENIA

CASPIAN SEA

AMIDA

EDESSA
CARRHAE

SASANIANS

HAMADAN

ANTIOCH
Libanius,
Ammianus

PALMYRA

CTESIPHON
Shapur

SUSA

DAMASCUS

EUPHRATES R.

BABYLON

TIGRIS R.

JERUSALEM

PERSIAN
GULF

CHAPTER I

Ferment and Repression

In this book I propose to deal with the epoch I call the Fourth Century. Purists will perhaps be outraged to discover that for me this is only a term of convenience since it is not the period 300-400 A.D. but one beginning in 324 with the sole reign of Constantine the Great and fading away with no precise end sometime before the death of Theodosius II in 450. This was certainly in the twilight of antiquity; some might also see it as the beginning of the Middle Ages, but I refuse to argue that point.

My Fourth Century was an eventful, lively era in which people were forced by special circumstances to make momentous decisions that determined the fortunes of mankind for centuries thereafter. Constantine's resolve to build a New Rome, to move his capital to Byzantium, led ultimately to the division of the Roman Empire into two parts—East and West—culturally the one, Greek; the other, Latin. His tacit abandonment of the West doomed it to barbarian occupation, while at the same time the concentration of power in the Greco-Oriental East facilitated the preservation of civilization even though later the region was split politically between the Byzantine Christians and the converts to Islam.

Again, because he emerged the victor in the struggle for the throne that followed the retirement of Diocletian in 305 and because he survived his rivals by more than a decade, Constantine's alliance with the Christians became a permanent arrangement rather than a temporary expedient. Its consequences were not only the formulation of a new theory of government by divine right, but also a wedding of church and state that was to have advantages and disadvantages for both partners. In the future neither would be quite the same as before.

The church-state combination necessitated a definition of orthodoxy. The emperor must take sides in the quarrels of the theologians; he must close the ranks of his divided new allies. Heresy thus became a crime against the state as well as against religion. This meant among other things that the Christians now had a chance to persecute one another in addition to being able to pay back the pagans in their own coin—with interest.

The demand for orthodoxy not only produced the Nicene Creed of 325 but also the formulation of the Canon of the New Testament which identified the genuine writings of early Christianity and excluded as apocrypha many books long accepted as sacred in numerous Christian communities. Moreover, the Old Testament came under examination, and when St. Jerome made his Latin translation later known as the Vulgate, he chose to follow the Hebrew text canonized by the Jews three centuries earlier and to omit material found in the Greek Old Testament, the Septuagint.

The move to Constantinople and the emperor's alliance with the Christians elevated the religious authorities at the new capital to unaccustomed heights much to the irritation of the metropolitans of Alexandria in Egypt, Antioch in Syria, and Old Rome in Italy. The Patriarch at Constantinople, destined to head the Greek church, was to engage over the centuries in a long series of contests with the Pope in Rome. Whatever their theological significance, these disputes were symbolic of the split between the Greek East and the Latin West.

Looking at other developments of the age, we see that monasticism was one of the most important with its formalization by St. Basil in the East and its diffusion to the West culminating in the Benedictine Rule two centuries later. Again, while one cannot truly characterize a certain trend as woman's liberation, our period was one in which women were more prominent in political and intellectual circles than they had been for some time. Among the great women of this era were the unfortunate Hypatia, philosopher, scientist, and mathematician; St. Helena, mother of Constantine, who after a somewhat chequered career became a pillar of the church; the indomitable Galla Placidia, daughter of Theodosius the Great, who was carried off from the sack of Rome to become the wife of the Visigoth Alaric and later wedded to the pretender, Constantius; Pulcheria, regent for Theodosius II; and Eudocia, the Athenian intellectual who married that same Theodosius.[1]

After the end of the Constantian dynasty, the barbarians became more troublesome, and the Romans fared less well against them on the battlefield in the fourth century than they had in the disastrous third. A mere listing of catastrophes will suffice: in the Battle of Adrianople in 378 the Goths destroyed a Roman army and killed the Emperor Valens; in 410 Alaric the Visigoth sacked Rome; as the Vandals overran North Africa, St. Augustine died in the siege of his city of Hippo (430). By the end of our period, Attila the Hun had appeared, and the Roman West had been invaded and occupied by Ostrogoths, Visigoths, Huns, Franks, Vandals, Burgundians, Saxons, Angles, and Jutes.

It was not just that the barbarians took territory from the empire and made it their own; even more distressing was the barbarian infiltration of the Roman army and the upper echelons of the government. Sometimes loyal beyond the call of duty, sometimes completely untrustworthy, the barbarians were everywhere and therefore bitterly resented by most Romans. A Stilicho or a Gainas had power but not popularity, nor did it help matters on either side that many of these foreigners were Arians—which made them heretics as well as savages.

The miracle was that the empire did not collapse. In spite of its trials and tribulations, it never came as close to the brink of extinction as it had in the third century. In fact, the fourth century by comparison with the third was a period of governmental stability and economic improvement. The clue to all this was dynastic continuity, sometimes reduced to a thin line but actually broken only once, and that briefly. From the Caesarship of Constantius, the father of Constantine, beginning in 293 to the death of Julian the Apostate seventy years later, the house of Constantius never lost its visibility; and from 364 to a quarter of a century beyond our period the dynasty founded by Valentinian and perpetuated by Theodosius the Great held sway. The names of all the rulers are familiar: Constantius Chlorus, Constantine the Great, Constantius II, Julian, Jovian, Valentinian, Valens, Theodosius the Great, Arcadius and Honorius, and the second Theodosius.

The foregoing review of the outstanding characteristics and developments of the Fourth Century serves, if nothing else, to demonstrate that the political, military, and religious history of the period is well-known, almost a matter of common knowledge, and has been treated in detail by more than a few really distinguished historians. Granting this, one might well ask whether there is anything more to be said, and the answer to that question is that the business of Clio is never finished. There are many different ways of looking at the past and so gaining a new understanding of it. Some approaches may prove more rewarding than others, but the historian, win or lose, is obligated to try more than one.

Let us suppose that for a bit we can turn away from the bloody shambles of the battlefields, away from the pomp and pretence of the court, away from the squalling of theological squabblers, and embark instead on a search for what I should like to call humanity. What can we learn about the people of the Fourth Century? What did they think was important, or good, or bad, or amusing? How did they see the period in which they lived? Can we reconstruct the atmosphere, character, or temper of this age? Are there attitudes or themes that run through the century that will give us its common denominator?

Where can we find the materials with which to reconstruct this vanished epoch? We shall have to cast a wide net. Although much that was written in our Fourth Century has survived, it alone will not suffice, and I do not intend a pun when I say that we shall leave no stone unturned because we shall indeed look at inscriptions and the monuments of architecture and sculpture. And this is not all. Let me give you a list and a few examples:

The literary (written) sources include the formal histories, of course. Among these the most famous are the works of Ammianus Marcellinus in Latin and Zosimus in Greek as well as the *Ecclesiastical History* of Eusebius and its continuation by later authors, both Latin and Greek. Theological works abound: Lactantius, St. Jerome, St. Augustine, and Sulpicius Severus lived and wrote in our period. There are philosophical tracts and commentaries. There are letters, orations, and treatises on a variety of subjects: medicine, strategy, science, technology, art, government, and statecraft. Nor can poetry be neglected, for the muse was courted by pagans and Christians alike.

A veritable mine of information is the Theodosian Code,[2] the compilation of imperial rescripts ordered by Theodosius II in 429 and completed in 438. It begins with the directives of Constantine the Great even before he became sole emperor, and, with the appended *Novels* of Theodosius, it carries us beyond the original date of compilation. Harsh and cruel in many of its penalites, it is strangely lenient in some cases; however, in general the growing tensions leading up to and after the Battle of Adrianople are reflected in an across-the-board crackdown aimed at promoting not merely orthodoxy but also regimentation and conformity.

Major crimes were defined as homicide, treason, adultery, incest, rape, infanticide, peculation, tomb robbing, practicing magic or sorcery, teaching astrology, and calling up demons.

Counterfeiting was in the beginning an offence punishable by loss of property, imprisonment, or banishment depending on the status of the offender; but it was later defined as high treason, and the guilty persons were burned alive. Also consigned to the flames were sorcerers, slaves who cohabited with free women, persons who harbored brigands, and anyone who assisted in rape. The rapist himself had molten lead poured down his throat. Parricides were sewed up in a sack with poisonous snakes and cast into the water. We also hear of such quaint little devices as the "torture horse" and the "iron claws"; the operational details of these machines are probably best left to the imagination. Branding, banishment, degradation even to slavery, a sentence to the mines or to servitude on an island were among the lesser penalties. Testimony in criminal cases was secured by torture although priests were exempt from such a radical procedure.

The Code shows clearly the major trends of the age. The Christians and their church made steady gains. If a man wished he might have his case tried in a church court presided over by a bishop even if the suit had already been instituted before a secular judge. The church could emancipate slaves, and churches became sanctuaries to which persons might flee from apprehension by the authorities. Laws penalizing unmarried and childless persons dating as far back as the time of Augustus were annulled by Constantine in 320 so that Christian celibates both male and female were emancipated from old penalties and permitted to receive inheritances.

No Christian could be enslaved by a Jew, nor could Jews marry Christian women. On the other hand, Jews were allowed freedom of worship, their synagogues were protected, synagogue officials were exempt from compulsory services, and no one could summon or bring suit against a Jew on the Sabbath. Heretics and pagans fared less well. The former were forbidden the right of assembly and were not allowed to form congregations. After the death of Julian the Apostate attacks on the pagans were mounted with increasing vigor. Long forbidden to perform sacrifices, the temples of the pagans were systematically dismantled, and "no one could revere an image formed by mortal labor."

A series of rescripts relating to holidays well illustrates the march of the Christian triumph. Constantine in 321 had made the Dies Solis, the Day of the Sun, a holiday. This was purposely ambiguous since it was a special day for both pagans and Christians. But before long Sunday was called the Lord's Day, and the Paschal Days, the seven before and the seven after Easter, became official holidays also. By the end of the century there were blue laws that forbade exhibitions in the circus on Sundays and outlawed Sunday horseracing and theatrical performances.

The growth of the autocracy and its creeping regimentation were reflected in many passages of the Code, typically in those rescripts that harnessed the *prudentes* and sought to bring the advocates under control. The glorious free-for-all of the jurisconsults, characteristic of the second and early third centuries, was ended, while those proud pleaders, the advocates, who sought to emulate Cicero and Pliny the Younger, were properly humbled. "We desire," said Constantine, "to eradicate the interminable controversies of the jurisconsults. We order the destruction of the notes of Ulpian and Paul upon Papinian, for, while they were eagerly pursuing praise for their genius, they preferred not so much to correct him as distort him."[3] An autocracy liked things neat and tidy and one-way. With a despot, there was little room for differences of opinion.

As for the advocates, the trial lawyers: "It has become increasingly evident that some advocates have preferred enormous and illicit profits to their own good reputation . . . there are advocates who consider not the right of a citizen's case but the quality and quantity of his farms, herds, and slaves and demand that the best part of such property shall be signed over to them by a forced pact. . . . If any person should wish to be an advocate, he shall assume only that one role in conducting cases. The same person cannot be advocate and judge in the same suit."[4]

Vignettes that give a glimpse of the times pop out of the pages of the Code. The decurions, the local senators or councillors, oppressed by the increasing responsibilities imposed upon them by the government, were becoming hard to find. They had fled: some into the underbrush of the bureaucracy; others became hermits, monks, ragmen, or philosophers. "Every man shall be returned to his municipality if he is recognized as having unduly and insolently usurped the garb of philosophers . . . for it is disgraceful that a man who professes to endure the violence of fortune cannot bear to perform the compulsory public duties of his municipality."[5] A truly desperate way of escape from compulsory service as a decurion, a real Hobson's choice, was to have thirteen children.

The autocracy also tightened its hold on the guilds: the breadmakers, the pack animal drivers, the swine collectors, the limeburners, the ragmen, the beggars, the collectors of purple dye fish, and so on. There was a freeze, not of prices or wages, but of occupations. "If any purple dye fish collector should forsake and despise the office of his own ignoble status . . . he shall be recalled to the bonds of his own profession and low birth status. . . . If any child has been born from a daughter of a purple dye fish collector . . . he shall assume the obligations of his mother's ignoble status."[6]

Slavery had been and continued to be an ugly fact of society. Captives of war were enslaved: "We grant to all persons the opportunity to supply their own fields with men of the aforesaid race," says a rescript of 409 referring to captives secured in a recent victory over the barbarians. The slaves in this instance could not be sold by the initial buyer until five years had elapsed, probably to discourage speculation in a tight labor market. Newborn children who had been abandoned (exposed) could be taken as slaves and could not be repossessed by their parents, "for no one can call his own a child whom he scorned when it was perishing." Slaves could be disciplined at the pleasure of their masters, of course. If slaves died from a beating, their masters were not held to account "if by the correction of very evil deeds they wished to obtain better conduct on the part of their household slaves.''

On the other hand, one is touched by the compassion of the emperor who forbade the mistreatment of the draft animals belonging to the public transportation system. The poor creatures were often beaten with clubs to make them go faster or even to move, and therefore the ruler ordered that "it is our pleasure that no person at all shall use a club in driving but shall employ either a switch or at the most a whip in the tip of which a short prick has been inserted by which the lazy limbs of the animals may be gently tickled into action."[7]

One could be as sure about the military as about death and taxes. The army was hard to get in if for some reason you wanted to join up and even harder to escape if you didn't. The sons of veterans were liable for military service, but some tried to avoid it by mutilating themselves. For this kind of evasion the penalties were harsh and got worse. "If they should be judged useless for service because their fingers have been cut off, we order them to be assigned to the performance of compulsory public services and duties of decurions."[8] Later, such offenders were consigned to the "avenging flames." It was not surprising that people tried to find substitutes who would stand in for them in the performance of military service—barbarians, veterans, or slaves. After 367, however, there was one sure escape from conscription: the army would take no one under 5 feet 7 inches tall.

As we shall see later, many of our sources in addition to the Code stress common themes: corruption in the bureaucracy, apprehensiveness with regard to the barbarians, concern for the improvement of technology, the prevalence of tomb robbing, and the almost universal resort to astrology and other forms of divination among Christians and pagans alike. According to the Code, it was wrong to employ the magic arts against the safety of mankind but proper to use them for cures of illness or to ensure good harvests. Ammianus has a revealing story about an emperor and a sort of ouija board:[9]

In 371 there was a plot, or so it was alleged, to assassinate the Emperor Valens. We shall never know the truth of the matter, and certainly little effort was made to discover the facts then. Accusations flew thick and fast. Many persons were convicted and executed—burned alive, torn to bits by hooks, or beheaded. One witness was burned alive when not enough of his body remained for further torture. Particularly interesting was the case of a certain Theodorus, a cultivated gentlemen without political aspirations. Two witnesses testified that they had constructed a model of the Delphic tripod out of laurel wood and placed upon it a circular metal plate engraved around its outer ring with the letters of the Greek alphabet. A diviner, after the proper ceremonies, then set in motion a hanging ring suspended by a linen thread which, in response to questions, spelled out on the board the answers in hexameter verse. When asked who would succeed the current emperor, the ring began with Theta and then passed successively to Epsilon, Omicron, and Delta. Further testimony was interrupted by the court of inquiry shouting that Theodorus was intended, and the poor man was sentenced to death on the spot.

History tells us that the actual successor of Valens was Theodosius. Clearly, the ouija board was infallible, and it was lucky for Theodosius that it was not allowed to tell its full story!

To come back to the chronic tomb robbing, some of it was aimed at carrying off the few poor possessions of the dead; sometimes tombs were demolished to get dressed stones for other buildings; occasionally, the burial places of the saints were ransacked to acquire relics for sale to the pious. All these motives were condemned by the Code, and guilty persons were threatened with severe punishment.

But the subject of the tombs brings us to another rich source of information: the sepulchral inscriptions in Latin, Greek, Hebrew, Coptic, and other languages of the empire. What can the gravestones tell us about the Fourth Century? A single inscription may reveal the status of the deceased, whether that person was a slave, SER(vus), a freedman L(ibertus), or a free man. Sometimes just the name will tell us this, and frequently we can ascertain whether he or she was a Roman, a Greek, or a barbarian and something about the country from whence the individual came. Occupations are often mentioned, and religious affiliations are usually plain enough. A pagan stone may use the abbreviation D. M. —*dis manibus*: to the gods of the underworld. Also common are H. S. E. —*Hic situs est*: he lies here; or S. T. T. L. —*Sit tibi terra levis*: light be the earth upon thee. A few examples from faraway Britain will suffice:

Aurelius Marcus erected a monument to his wife who lived thirty-three years *sine ulla macula* (without stain). She came from Salona in Dalmatia (Jugoslavia). Barates from Palmyra in Syria set up a stone for his wife, Regina, a British girl who was also his freedwoman and died at thirty. Flavius Antigonos Papias, a Greek, died at the age of sixty; his wife, who survived him, provided his tombstone. "I died many times but never like this," reads the sepulchral inscription of Leburna, the actor, who lived a full hundred years. Nor can we pass over the heart-rending case of little Fortunatus, age eight, who drowned in a fishpond.

Burials of Jews are often found grouped in separate cemetaries, but usually the names are distinctive enough to identify them as are the symbols engraved on the stones: the shofar, the menora, the cucurbita, the ark of the covenant, and so on. The titles of officials of the synagogue are given, or a convert will be designated as *proselitus*. The inscriptions may be in Latin, Greek, or Hebrew. *Bene merente* or *bene merente fecit* are common and so also are *in pace* or *en eirene*. One text reads *in pace et irene*, which seems a little redundant. *Shalom* is common, of course. A curious Latin inscription written in Greek characters reads (in transliteration) *Oulpia Mareina Kouai bixit anneis KB bene meraintis phekit*. A bilingual text says in Greek, "This is the tomb of Pareris," and in Hebrew, "Peace over Israel. Amen." One should not neglect to mention the stone of Veturia Paulina, *femina*, who lived eighty-six years, six months, was a proselyte sixteen years and was renamed Sara, Mother of the Synagogue.

Christian tombstones often have the chi rho monogram, or chi rho flanked by alpha and omega. Common symbols are the palm, a column, an olive branch, the crown and column, calix and cross, the anchor, or the fish (*ichthus*). *In agape* (in love), *cum pace*, *R.I.P.*, "he lived in this world," "he is freed from human cares," "he departed the body," and so on are common phrases. Married persons will record that they lived together *sine bile* or *sine ulla quaerella* (without a quarrel).

The stones are often dated, usually by the names of the eponymous *consules ordinarii* or by indictions. Not only are we told in some cases the age of the deceased in years but also in months, days, and even hours. Moreover, by the fourth century we are frequently given the precise month and day of the week when the subject departed this life, and we thus have in addition a clear indication that the concept of the seven-day week, an eastern import, has finally been adopted in the west: its days are those of the Moon, Mars, Mercury, Jove, Venus, Saturn, and the Sun, the list every beginning student of French knows as Lundi, Mardi, Mercredi, etc.

As one might suspect, something can be done with vital statistics through a study of the gravestones. From a hasty survey of some 650 texts it would appear that a third of those born in my Fourth Century did not live ten years, one-half never made it to twenty, and another 15 percent died before thirty. Three-fourths of the population was under forty. Only 5 percent of those born in any given year could expect to reach sixty-five. Of the number surveyed, five persons lived to be over ninety, and one lasted over a century; but it was essentially a young population. Unfortunately, we do not know in most cases what carried them off. Infant mortality and the death rate of women in childbirth were high. Wars and plagues accounted for many, but they were not bothered by some of our modern killers: nobody smoked too many cigarettes, the chariot death toll was nowhere near one a day per province, and they lacked such population regulators as motorcycles and snowmobiles.

As a numismatist it pains me to confess that the coinage of the Fourth Century is less versatile in its capacity for historical testimony than the issues of the early Roman Empire. Commemorative issues are rare; there seems to be less use of the coins as a vehicle for imperial propaganda; varieties of types and legends are quite limited. The fourth-century coins do tell us something about the artistic trends of the period; they provide portraits of the emperors; and they are invaluable as evidence for the fluctuating fortunes of the economy. This, regrettably, just about exhausts the list.

As we turn to other types of visual, physical, archaeological evidence—architectural monuments, sculpture, painting, mosaics—it is perhaps best for each of us first to look at these materials without preconceptions derived from the opinions of others. That there is a new style is apparent, and it is also clear that new methods and techinques have been introduced: the plain, rather monotonous exteriors of the buildings contrasting with the elaborateness of the interiors, the use of the chisel replaced by that of the running drill, and much more.

I have neither the courage nor the competence to try to make the kind of subjective judgments about these things that might be made by an art historian, but I do find the conclusions of the Norwegian scholar H. P. L'Orange extremely interesting and provocative.[10] L'Orange finds parallel developments in the autocracy and art although it should be noted that he is very careful to state that these are parallels and not necessarily related. If I may paraphrase his remarks, he says that with the increasing standardization and equalization of life, the block-like fusion of civic organization, there was no place for individualism. We can perhaps see this in the reliefs in which crowds of people are shown participating in imperial ceremonies and the like; they have, I would agree, no more individuality than the clumps of flowers in a painting or a photograph of a formal garden. Architecture, says L'Orange, became introspective. The prime function of a building was to act as an enclosure of space. People turned to the abstract, and the abstraction in art symbolized the whole attitude of the age toward every phase of existence. In the portraits the eye is directed toward a new goal. It looks past the elusive, discordant physical world and immerses itself in the higher absolutes, the unchangeable symmetry, of the realm of eternity. The massive all-absorbing formations in the life of state and society correspond to the distinctive, compact form creations in contemporary architecture and art. There is a movement toward the simple, from the mobile to the static, from the dialectic and relative toward the dogmatic and authoritarian, from the empirical toward theology and theosophy, and these trends in the Late Empire are paralleled in figurative art which moves away from the animated forms of nature to a firm and inflexible typology, from body to symbol.

I myself cannot help wondering how we would interpret the art of the fourth century if we knew nothing of the autocracy and the new way of life that it brought, and I have not forgotten what Rhys Carpenter once said about this problem:

It is a very popular notion—strangely compounded of clairvoyance and prejudice—that art invariably reflects the civilization that produced it. The progress of art is too slow and too deep a stream to offer more than mere surface reflections to the casual spectator. Casually and trivially, much of the contemporary world may thus be imaged; but if one would discover any very significant correspondence between art and life, one must penetrate beneath the running surface.[11]

◇◇◇◇◇◇◇◇◇◇◇◇◇◇

These are the sources. We can use or misuse them. No one would deliberately twist the evidence to support a preconceived point of view, but we shall not get the right answers if we ask the wrong questions. As we proceed I shall give you the facts and my interpretations of them, yet you should not be so docile as to accept my ideas without testing them or working to formulate opinions of your own.

We have already skated around the subjectivity of the art historians, but we cannot avoid subjective judgments of our own when it comes to historical interpretation. Let none think that the present can be escaped by diving into the past. For us, the past is often the mirror of the present because the past will only reflect what we ourselves know or feel in the light of our own experience. Less than a generation ago our view of the Fourth Century would probably have been quite different from what it is now. This is because of the new and unpredictable things we have experienced in recent years, and this is also one reason why historical interpretation is open-ended and will always be so. The techniques of science may aid historical research, but they will never make history itself a science. History is a discipline, to be sure. Yet in its highest and truest form it is contemplative and literary rather than scientific.

In one of Jane Austen's novels there is this dialogue between two ladies:

"I can read poetry and plays, and things of that sort, and do not dislike travels. But history, real solemn history, I cannot be interested in. Can you?"

"Yes, I am fond of history."

"I wish I were, too. I read it a little as a duty, but it tells me nothing that does not either vex or weary me. The quarrels of popes and kings, with wars and pestilences, in every page. The men are all so good for nothing, and hardly any women at all—it is very tiresome; and yet I think it odd that it should be so dull, for a great deal of it must be invention."

"Historians, you think," said Miss Tilney, "are not happy in their flights of fancy. They display imagination without arousing interest. I am fond of history—and am very well contented to take the false with the true. In the principal facts they have sources of intelligence in former histories and records, which may be as much depended on, I conclude, as anything that does pass under one's own observation; and as for the little embellishments you speak of, they are embellishments, and I like them as such."[12]

Finally, to illustrate what I was saying a moment ago about the topicality of historical interpretation, let me suggest this:

The Fourth Century gives more than a superficial impression of having been much like our present. It began as a period of ferment and rebellion. Within the framework of every religious group, for example, there might be found dissidence, disagreement, and fragmentation, and a like situation prevailed within the philosophical sects. The approach to problems tended to be emotional rather than intellectual. Often the occult took precedence over reason. Good intentions and a kind of missionary fervor in problem solving were preferred to a basic knowledge of the subject at hand buttressed by study and reflection. There was a general rejection of the old ways, a contempt for tradition. There was a decline of discipline. There was immense fear of the barbarians (i.e., foreigners) who had gained not only technological equality with the Romans but military superiority as well.

Echoes from the Theodosian Code have a familiar ring. There are sections relating to urban renewal, pollution, price freezing, a shortage of trained workers, socialized medicine, and passages like the following:

"We command that no person shall be allowed to wear long hair."

"Within the city of Rome no person shall wear either trousers or boots —he should clothe himself with the sober robes of everyday costume."

"Students should conduct themselves in their assemblies as persons who should consider it their duty to avoid a disgraceful and scandalous reputation and bad associations."

We know that this was a dying civilization. Were these its outstanding characteristics? We also know that ferment was followed by repression, by a forced closing of the ranks, and by autocracy. Could this have any sort of message for us?

This is not the time to accept or reject any of this speculation since there will be ample opportunity to test it in the future. In the meantime we shall prosecute our search for humanity, forsaking popes and kings, wars and pestilences, and strive to learn something about some of the representative people of the Fourth Century. Using our sources, we shall travel the length and breadth of the empire and from the top to the bottom of society as we examine the careers and opinions of individuals who lived in our period. Some famous or infamous persons will cross our path and some very ordinary ones. The exigence of selection will prevent us from becoming better acquainted with Constantine or Theodosius or with such characters as St. Martin, the boorish bishop of Tours, or George of Cappadocia, butcher, bishop, and bibliophile, or the crafty Arius who might have been St. Arius with a little luck, and many more.

We shall find our common denominators, never fear, but most important I shall hope that you will recognize the powerful bond of humanity that unites us with these friends and neighbors of so long ago.

CHAPTER II

The Pilgrim

The growth of Christian pilgrimage is one of the outstanding features of the fourth century. It was not included in our earlier list of things characteristic of the period because then we were concentrating on matters of more or less common knowledge. Pilgrimage, on the other hand, is not so familiar but it is still important and interesting enough to merit some discussion. Although the subject itself is not generally regarded as controversial, there is, as you will see, ample room for a difference of opinion.

Pilgrim is almost a charged word and has been so for a long time. What with our Pilgrim Fathers and all the rest of it, people have made assumptions about the very early pilgrims that deserve to be challenged. Perhaps we should look at the facts and try to see what they suggest.

Etymologically a pilgrim is a wayfarer or traveler, a sojourner, a bird of passage, or a foreigner. In ancient times the word *peregrinus* (pilgrim) lacked the favorable connotation, the odor of sanctity and respect, that it now has. When Catiline called Cicero a *peregrinus* he intended no compliment. When Lucian satirized a notorious second-century charlatan he chose to name him Peregrine and described him as a type of flim-flam man (though somewhat lacking the amusing and

human qualities of the movie character as portrayed by George
C. Scott).

The fourth-century pilgrim was not the stereotype we often
associate with the Middle Ages. He or she went to Jerusalem
and the Holy Land, not to Rome or to some regional shrine.
Erase, too, from your mind the picture of the dusty, weary
traveler clutching a staff as he plods along on foot. Most of
our fourth-century friends went first class. The Pilgrim of
333, whose account is the earliest known, obviously did not
travel on foot as the relative speed of his progress demonstrates.
Egeria, or whatever her name was, rated a military escort in the
tight places and got a lot of attention from important people
wherever she went. Paula was a Roman noblewoman inspired
to pilgrimage by St. Jerome, the Henry Ward Beecher of his
age. Her hosts were bishops and archbishops, and when she
arrived in Jerusalem the Roman proconsul swept out the praetorium for her. From such evidence we might be tempted to
imagine that pilgrimage was the prerogative of the Roman jet
set.

But let us not jump to conclusions. The evidence will not
fully justify the flippant suggestion I have just made; neither
does it support the usual sobersided, straightfaced approach.
We have only four documents: the itinerary of the Bordeaux
pilgrim of 333; the incomplete letter of Egeria from about 381;
the letter of Paula and Eustochium to Marcella; and St. Jerome's effusion entitled "The Pilgrimage of the Holy Paula."[1]
The account by the Bordeaux pilgrim is brief and matter-of-
fact; Egeria is ingenuous and obviously sincere; Paula often
sounds like a modern celebrity on a protracted holiday. Nevertheless, from these four documents certain reasonable deduc-
tions can be made. The Bordeaux Itinerary presupposes pre-
vious as well as quite a bit of contemporary pilgrimage. It is
the earliest surviving account but not necessarily the first of
its kind. There was already enough traffic so that people were
desirous of having some such guidebook for their travels. If
we compare the Itinerary and the accounts of Egeria and Paula,

it becomes very plain also that within half a century there had been a proliferation of holy sites for pilgrims to visit and a wealth of relics to buy as souvenirs. If you wanted a sliver of the True Cross discovered by St. Helena, the mother of Constantine, there was no problem. It must have been a very big one to have supplied the wants of so many people, and it is also worth noting that Helena's discovery was unknown to her immediate contemporaries.

Persons more cynical than you or I might say that all this has an air of tourism, but we must always be careful not to interpret the past in terms of the present—if we can help it. Neither would it be fair to quote the following passage out of context. It comes from St. Jerome's "Pilgrimage of the Holy Paula." At Samaria Paula visited the tombs of Elijah, Obadiah, and John the Baptist. At the last site "she trembled at many wonders, for she beheld demons roaring with various torments, and, before the sepulchre of the saints, men who howled like wolves, barked with the voices of dogs, roared with those of lions, hissed like serpents, bellowed like bulls, while others turned round their heads and touched the ground behind their backs with the crown of their heads, and women hung by their feet with their clothes flowing over their faces."[2] There must have been a Fun House or a Tunnel of Love, too, but Jerome does not mention it.

Enough of that. Let us be serious and start at the beginning. The Bordeaux Itinerary is representative of a type of compilation much older than Greece or Rome. Such road guides were available for traders and the military from very early times. Babylonian traders in the days of Hammurabi used them, and in the classical period similar data provided a partial source for the geographical accounts of Strabo and Pliny the Elder. People also made maps. We have Sumerian field plans on clay tablets dating before 2000 B.C. and city and area maps from the second millennium of the pre-Christian era. The idea of the *periplus* or *itinerarium maritimum* came to the Greeks from the Phoenicians. In Roman times Augustus ordered the drafting and

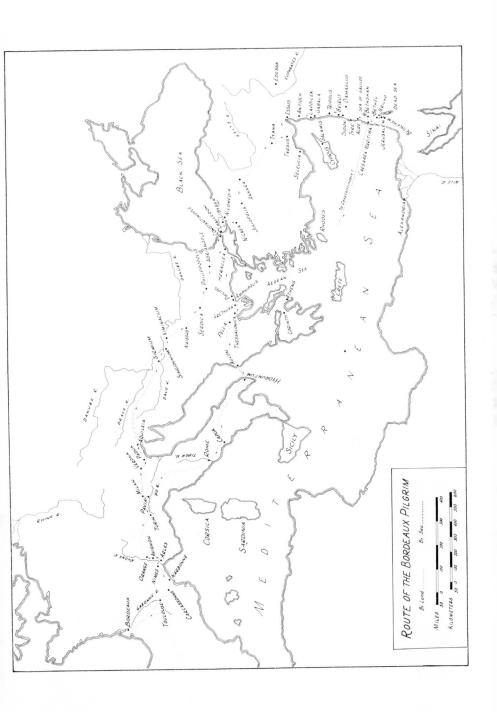

ROUTE OF THE BORDEAUX PILGRIM

By Land ————
By Sea ----------

MILES 50 0   100   200   300   400
KILOMETERS 50 0   100   200   300   400   500   600

BLACK SEA

MEDITERRANEAN SEA

AEGEAN SEA

RHINE R.

DANUBE R.

DRAVE R.

SAVE R.

TIBER R.

PO R.

RHONE R.

GARONNE R.

DANUBE R.

CORSICA

SARDINIA

SICILY

CRETE

CYPRUS

SINAI

NILE R.

EUPHRATES R.

BORDEAUX
TOULOUSE
CARCASSONNE
NARBONNE
NIMES
ARLES
AVIGNON
ORANGE
TURIN
PAVIA
MILAN
AQUILEIA
VERONA
BRESCIA

SIRMIUM
SINGIDUNUM
VIMINACIUM
NAISSUS
SERDICA
PHILIPPOPOLIS
ADRIANOPLE
HERACLEA
CONSTANTINOPLE

CAPUA
CANUSIUM
ROME

HYDRUNTUM

AULON
THESSALONICA
PELLA
ARETHUSA
AMPHIPOLIS
NEAPOLIS

CORINTH
ATHENS

NICOMEDIA
LIBYSSA
NICAEA
JULIOPOLIS
ANCYRA

TYANA
TARSUS
SELEUCIA
ISSUS
ANTIOCH
LAODICEA
GABALA
TRIPOLIS
BEIRUT
DAMASCUS
SIDON
TYRE
ACRE
SEA OF GALILEE
BETHSAN
CAESAREA MARITIMA
JERUSALEM
BETHLEHEM
JERICHO
DEAD SEA

EDESSA

ALEXANDRIA

RHODES

SALAMIS

To Constantinople

To Constantinople

public display of a huge map of the whole empire, and we also have fragments of a city map of Rome. Mile posts dotted the roads of the Roman Empire giving the distances from A to B in *millia passuum*, thousands of double paces. The double pace was about five English feet so that a Roman mile, 1,000 double paces, was shorter than the English mile by nearly 100 yards. In other words, eighteen Roman miles would be roughly equivalent to seventeen English miles.

Itineraria, Roman road guides, go back to the third century A.D. and probably earlier. The Antonine Itinerary,[3] the oldest we have, seems to date from the late third century because it mentions a place called Diocletianopolis. It lists post roads and mileages beginning in North Africa, then working through Sardinia, Corsica, Sicily, and Italy proceeding to the Roman East and back again ending in Britain. It also includes the sea routes. A half-dozen manuscripts of the Antonine Itinerary survive; the earliest dates from the seventh century and the latest from the fifteenth. By combining all the manuscripts, a virtually complete restoration of the text is possible.

The Bordeaux Itinerary of 333 is much like the Antonine guide except that it was devised for pilgrims who wanted to go to the Holy Land from the West. Furthermore, it has a few notes here and there about places of interest along the way and even more information, of course, about what to see in Palestine. The earliest surviving manuscript is of the ninth century; only a few others are extant, nothing like the six for the Antonine text. It is worth noting that the route of the Bordeaux pilgrim does not use the roads defined as the main highways in the Antonine Itinerary. This is hard to understand except that we know that many routes were repaired and put in service between 284 and 333 A.D. Moreover, the Antonine guide could be based on a much earlier, lost original.

Both the Antonine and Bordeaux itineraries are rather bland and prosaic when compared with the Peutinger Table, a road map antedating 400 A.D.[4] The surviving copy is an illuminated manuscript of the fourth century *one foot wide and twenty-one feet long*. It has no recognizable scale but begins at the Atlantic —that section is missing—and goes not only to the Near East but even on to India, not neglecting the Holy Land, of course. Rome and Constantinople are naturally given top billing. It is interesting and instructive that the routes are not precisely the same as those of the Antonine or Bordeaux guides.

Coming back to the Bordeaux pilgrim, his account is more complete and detailed than those of Egeria and Paula with regard to the routes to be followed and the circumstances of the journey, but they have more to say about the Holy Land, the goal of the venture. In addition, the point is often made that the Bordeaux pilgrim was not aware of as many of the Christian holy places as his successors fifty years later. The majority of the sites he mentions are Old Testament ones; fewer are connected with the New Testament. He went to Jerusalem, of course, and to Bethlehem, but not to Nazareth. Instead, he visited Jericho and the Dead Sea.

The Bordeaux pilgrim's journey took him 7,000 miles in the space of nearly two years. On the road he averaged less than twenty-five miles a day, but this was partly due to rough terrain in some places. His journey from Constantinople to Jerusalem and return which he estimates at something over 2,000 miles lasted from May 30 to Christmas Day. Four of these seven months were spent on the road; the remainder of the period was devoted to sightseeing.

The long pilgrimage began at Bordeaux, or as he says "from Burdigala where the river Garumna (Garonne) in which the ocean ebbs and flows for 100 leagues." The league in this case is the Gallic one equivalent to one and one-half Roman miles, and it is the unit of measurement used by the pilgrim on the first stage of his journey from Bordeaux to Toulouse. After that Roman miles were used. It is interesting that 400 years after Julius Caesar the people of southern Gaul, Romanized as they were, had not forgotten their past. The native dialects were known and still spoken by some people, and as we see here the old system of measurement by Gallic leagues was still in use.

In the Bordeaux Itinerary the stopping places and the distances between them are given. The stopping places are of two kinds: the *mutationes*, post stations at which fresh horses are secured, and the points that mark the end of each day's journey. Such termini are at a *civitas* (city), *vicus* (town), or a *mansio* (probably more like what we used to call a tourist home before the day of the motel). The only other term designating a site along the road is *castellum* (fortress).

The pilgrim's log for the first day of his trip reads: "from Bordeaux: change at Stomatae, 7 leagues; change at Senone, 9 leagues; stop at *civitas* of Vasates, 8 leagues." The first leg, then, covered about thirty-four English miles; the next day went better (three changes, forty miles); the third day, not so well (two changes, less than thirty miles); but on the fourth day by some real pushing the pilgrim covered the remaining fifty miles to Toulouse. He had journeyed more than 150 miles in four days, but it was to take eight more days to travel the 200-plus miles from Toulouse to Arles.

The pilgrim has nothing to say about the towns of Gaul through which he passed, probably because he assumed that his readers would know them. Fortunately for us, Ausonius the poet, no pilgrim and apparently not much of a Christian, was a native of Bordeaux and in his poems describes some of the Gallic towns. Ausonius was born in Bordeaux, where his father was a physician, in 310. He had gone to school in Bordeaux and later at Toulouse, but by the time the pilgrim was setting out, Ausonius had returned to Bordeaux to teach as a *grammaticus* and to practice law. About the time the pilgrim returned from Jerusalem, Ausonius was getting married. Fame and fortune for Ausonius were still about thirty years away when he would become the tutor of the future emperor Gratian, rise eventually to the consulship, and be the intimate of important pagan intellectuals in Rome. We shall meet Ausonius again, but for the moment we shall see what he has to say about southern Gaul, the region through which the pilgrim was passing.

Ausonius lists Bordeaux last in his catalogue of famous cities, but he makes up for it:

> Long have I censured my unduteous silence in that of thee, my country famed for thy wine, thy rivers, thy famous men, the virtue and wit of thy inhabitants . . . for mine is no barbarous land. . . . Bordeaux is my native soil, where skies are temperate and mild, and well-watered land, generously lavish, where is long spring and winters growing warm with the new-born sun, and tidal rivers whose flood foams beneath vine-clad hills, mimicking the ocean's ebb and flow. Her goodly walls four-square raise lofty towers . . . within her, thou mayest marvel at streets clearly laid out, at houses regularly plotted, at spacious boulevards. . . . This is my own country, but Rome stands above all countries. I love Bordeaux; Rome I venerate; in this I am a citizen; in both a consul; here was my cradle; there my curule chair.[5]

Or again, of Toulouse: "my nursing mother, who is girt about with a vast circuit of brick-built walls, along whose side the lovely stream of the Garonne glides past."[6]

Or of Narbonne, the pilgrim's second major terminus:

"Nor shalt thou be unsung, Martian Narbonne, who gav'st thy name to that province . . . in all Gaul the first to display the insignia of the Roman race. . . . What shall I say of thy harbors, mountains, lakes . . . or of the temple of Parian marble so vast in bulk. The merchandise of the Eastern Sea and Spain enrich you and all cargo passing by many different routes over rivers and seas."[7]

The pilgrim next passed through Nemausus (Nimes) and then came to Arelate (Arles) on the Rhone. "Arelate," says Ausonius, "the little Rome of Gaul . . . divided by the headlong Rhone thy central street made of a bridge of boats."[8]

From Arles the pilgrim went north through Avignon, Orange, and ultimately crossed the Alps, descended into Italy, then made his way through Turin and Pavia to Milan where he arrived three weeks after leaving Arles. "At Milan also are all things wonderful, abundant wealth, countless stately houses, men able, eloquent and cheerfully disposed . . . the Circus, the enclosed theatre with wedge-like blocks of seats, the temples, the imperial citadels, the mint and the quarter (called) the Baths of Hercules (named for Maximian, colleague of Diocletian and father-in-law of Constantius Chlorus)."[9]

Leaving Milan, the pilgrim moved through northern Italy by way of Verona and Padua, and after nine days came to Aquileia. From thence he went over the Julian Alps to the Drave River "where," he says, "you cross a bridge and enter Lower Pannonia." It took five weeks to go from Aquileia to Sirmium, and then the route lay through Singidunum (Belgrade), Viminiacium "where Diocletian killed Carinus," Naissus (Nish, birthplace of Constantine though not mentioned as such), Serdica (Sophia), Philippopolis, Heraclea, and at last, Constantinople, nearly 2,200 miles from Bordeaux involving a total journey of more than three months. Since the pilgrim was to press on from Constantinople toward Jerusalem at the end of May, he must have set out from Bordeaux in February. It seems odd that he has no remarks to make about Constantinople, dedicated in 330, only three years before his arrival, but again he may have felt that the imperial capital was well known and did not require explanation or comment.

"From Constantinople," says the pilgrim, "you cross the strait, come to Chalcedon, and travel through the province of Bithynia." Just as since leaving Italy he had followed the great military roads that had echoed to the tread of Roman legions, marching, countermarching, to defend the empire or to support one pretender to the throne against another, so now the pilgrim stayed on the main highway. About twenty-five miles into Bithynia he came to Libyssa where he notes, "Here lies King Annibalianus who was once King of the Africans." Clearly, the pilgrim was not up on his ancient history, for this was the tomb of Hannibal, his last refuge from pursuit by Romans, Seleucids, and his own Carthaginians.

The pilgrim next passed through Nicomedia (formerly Diocletian's capital) and Nicaea, both cities well known from the letters of Pliny the Younger and the orations of Dio Chrysostom. Turning east, the route led through Juliopolis to Ankara where our traveler probably saw the temple of Roma and Augustus bearing the Greek and Latin texts of the Res Gestae. The pilgrim was now two weeks out from Constantinople and soon turned southeast through Ozizala (later in St. Basil's country) and on to Tyana, "the home of Apollonius the magician," the wonder-worker immortalized by Philostratus, though in Tyana the services of Philostratus as a press agent were hardly needed to perpetuate the memory of Apollonius—everyone knew that at least a century and a half after his death Apollonius had returned from the great beyond to scare the Emperor Aurelian right out of his purple chlamys![10]

From Tyana the road went south through the famous Cilician Gates to Tarsus, the hometown of St. Paul (as noted by the pilgrim), then around the Gulf of Alexandretta to Issus, where Alexander had captured the queen and harem of Darius III, and so on to Syrian Antioch, the Fair Crown of the Orient. Forty days had passed since the pilgrim had left Constantinople. It was now July and probably very warm as he followed the coastal route via Gabala, Balaneas, and Antaradus where "is a city in the sea, two miles from the shore." This was the old Phoenician city state, and the pilgrim was to pass through others: Beirut, Sidon, Tyre, Acre. Then he crossed over Mt. Carmel, entered Palestine, and arrived at Caesarea Maritima two weeks after leaving Antioch. "At the third milestone from Caesarea," he says, "there is a fountain in which if a woman bathes, she becomes pregnant." He was now proceeding east toward Bethshan, and about two-thirds of the way there he notes, "Here is the field where David slew Goliath."

South from Bethshan was the land of Joseph and Jacob. The pilgrim saw Joseph's tomb; the place where Jacob dug the well; and where also Jesus talked with the woman of Samaria —"and there are plane trees which Jacob planted." Then came Bethar (Bethel) "where Jacob wrestled with the angel" and "here was King Jeroboam when the prophet was sent to him that he should turn himself to the Most High God; and the prophet was ordered not to eat bread with the false prophet which the king had with him, and because he was beguiled by the false prophet and ate bread with him, as he was returning a lion fell upon the prophet on the way and slew him."[11]

Finally, Jerusalem—two months after leaving Constantinople, five months since the departure from Bordeaux. It was August. The pilgrim saw Bethesda "where persons who have been sick many years are cured" and a "crypt where Solomon used to torture devils" as well as "the corner of a high tower where our Lord ascended and the tempter said to him 'If thou be the Son of God, cast thyself down from thence!'" He visited the site of Solomon's temple and "the altar before which the blood of Zacharias which was shed upon the stone pavement remains to this day and there are also to be seen the marks of the nails in the shoes of the soldiers who slew him . . . so plain you would think they were impressed upon wax."[12] Nearby were two statues of Hadrian who refounded Jerusalem as the Roman colony of Aelia Capitolina. Then to Zion and below "a spring which runs six days and nights but not on the Sabbath." Our traveler also saw the site of the palace of David, the gate of Neapolis where was the praetorium of Pontius Pilate, and on the left "the little hill of Golgotha where the Lord was crucified," and close by the vault where his body was laid "and rose again on the third day." Here Constantine had just completed a basilica, "a church of wondrous beauty." At the ascent to the Mount of Olives one could see a stone where Judas Iscariot betrayed Christ, and a palm tree from which the children took branches to strew in the way "as Christ came." Nearby were the tombs of Isaiah, the prophet, and Hezekiah, King of the Jews.

On the way to Jericho, the pilgrim passed "the sycamore tree into which Zacchaeus climbed that he might see Christ," and at Jericho itself was the fountain of Elishah, where if any woman drank she did not bear children, as well as the house of the harlot Rahab who protected the spies of Joshua. Of the Dead Sea the pilgrim remarked, "The water is very bitter and in it there is no kind of fish whatever . . . and if a man casts himself into it in order to swim, the water turns him over."[13] In Bethlehen "where our Lord Jesus Christ was born" he saw another basilica built by Constantine, and he finished his tour in Hebron "where is a monument of wondrous beauty in which lie Abraham, Isaac, Jacob, Sarah, Rebecca, and Leah."

The pilgrim then returned to Caesarea Maritima and may have proceeded from thence to Constantinople by sea. After this he followed another great military road across Macedonia and Greece to the Adriatic passing through Philippi, Amphipolis, Arethusa ("where is buried Euripides"), Thessalonica, and Pella ("whence came Alexander the Great"). The road ended at Aulon where he embarked to cross the Adriatic, "a thousand stadia which makes one hundred miles," to Hydryntum (Otranto). Moving to Capua, "mighty in tillage and in fruits, in luxury, in wealth," on the other side of the Italian peninsula, the pilgrim went on to Rome where he arrived two months after departing from Constantinople. Three weeks later he was in Milan, the last stop he records. Presumably he retraced his route from Milan to Bordeaux.

Fifty years after the Bordeaux pilgrim, a nun named Egeria, Aetheria, or perhaps Silvia made a three-year pilgrimage to the Holy Land and Egypt. We do not know where she originated, perhaps Spain or Gaul, and we lack the full story of her travels: only the fragment of a letter written to her sister nuns back home remains. This in turn comes from a single manuscript, copied at Monte Cassino in the eleventh century, although the complete version was still available and used at Monte Cassino by Peter the Deacon a hundred years later, and a Spanish priest is known to have seen a copy of Egeria's letter as early as the seventh century.

The fragment we possess comes at the very end of the account, telling how Egeria left Palestine and made her way after several detours back to Constantinople. Before starting for home Egeria decided to make a trip (her second) to Egypt and to visit Mt. Sinai on the way. Typically for her, she was not content to look at the mountain but insisted on climbing to its very peak. "The church which is now there," she says, "is not impressive for its size—there is too little room on the summit—but it has a grace all its own. And when with God's help we had climbed right to the top and reached the door of this church, there was a priest . . . coming to meet us from his cell. He was a healthy old man and an ascetic as they call it here—in fact just the man for the place."[14]

As she surveyed the monasteries and monks of the eastern Delta in Egypt, Egeria met a bishop whom she had encountered on her first trip: "He is a holy man, a true man of God. This holy bishop had been a monk, brought up in a cell since boyhood, and this is how he came to know so much about the Bible, and to live the faultless life I have mentioned."[15]

Having climbed Sinai, nothing would do but that before Egeria returned from the Egyptian venture and was about to leave Palestine for good she should ascend Mt. Nebo, across the Jordan east of Jericho, where Moses had been allowed to see the Promised Land. This was her recollection of that visit:

> On reaching the mountain top we came to a church, not a very big one right on the summit of Mt. Nebo, and inside in the position of the pulpit, I saw a slightly raised place about the size of a normal tomb. I asked about it and the holy men replied, 'Holy Moses was buried here by angels, since the Bible tells us *No human being knoweth his burial.* And there is no doubt that it was angels who buried him, since the actual tomb where he was buried can be seen today. Our predecessors here pointed out the place to us, and now we point it out to you.' They told us that this tradition came from their predecessors.[16]

On the way to Constantinople Egeria felt compelled to make a side trip eastward from Syrian Antioch to Edessa to visit the tomb of the apostle Thomas, twenty-five staging posts from Jerusalem. Moreover, the vicinity was swarming with innumerable holy monks and contained other notable items in addition to the martyrium of Thomas. Most impressive was the palace of that King Abgar who was reputed to have invited Jesus to come and abide with him. Not only did the local bishop show Egeria the palace and a marvelous portrait of Agbar, he also acquainted her with Agbar's letter and the response of Jesus who regretfully declined the invitation but promised to send one of his disciples instead. Apparently, copies of the two letters were available and often presented to devout visitors, for Egeria came away with these souvenirs.

Seven staging posts from Antioch was Tarsus in Cilicia, and Egeria might have gone by the normal route northward from there through the Cilician Gates, but she was bent on another detour. Three staging posts to the east, the route passsing through Pompeiopolis and Corycus, was Seleucia, the site of the tomb of the "holy Thecla." There Egeria was delighted to see once more a deaconess called Marthana whom she had met in Jerusalem.

Even after finally reaching Constantinople, the lively Egeria was not finished. At the end of her epistle she announces that she is going to Ephesus to see the tomb of the apostle John, and "if after that I am still alive, and able to visit further places, I will either tell you about them face to face (if God so wills), or at any rate write to you about them if my plans change."[17]

One final footnote on Sister Egeria—she does not seem to have been St. Silvia of Aquitaine as some people once suspected. Silvia was tough, hard as nails, a complete ascetic, a Carrie Nation type who was also a dirty old woman, for she once said:

> I am now sixty years of age; but except the tips of my fingers no water has ever touched my face, or my feet, or any of my limbs. Even when being seized with various diseases, I was urged by the physicians to take a bath, I could not endure to give the flesh its due. I have never slept on a couch or traveled anywhere in a litter.[18]

Like Silvia, who was the sister of the Prefect Rufinus, the Holy Paula was also of the nobility; but there the likeness ends. Paula hobnobbed with the great and mighty, entertained bishops in her home, and came late to pilgrimage. She was about thirty-five when she got the call, and one might guess that it came after the death of her husband by whom she had at least three children. His name was Toxotius, but otherwise he remains obscure. At any rate, about the same time that Egeria was in the Holy Land, Paula arrived there, although the two never met. Paula sailed from Ostia, the port of Rome, to Antioch in Syria, and then traveled aboard a donkey to Palestine. She left behind in Rome a young son, a daughter who was about to be married—Paula would not even stay for the wedding—and she took with her a spinster daughter named Eustochium who later became a bride of Christ. On the way to Palestine, Paula reaped the fruits of her hospitality in Rome by visiting Bishop Epiphanius of Salamis in Cyprus and Bishop Paulinus in Antioch.

The two-year pilgrimage of Paula was a grand tour with Roman officials and high dignitaries of the church turning out at every stage of the journey. Part of the reason for this was that Paula was important, but another part was that she had turned all her property into ready cash. Her resources must have been considerable because everywhere she went people were not left empty-handed. For example, on ascending Zion she was shown "a column supporting the portico of a church, stained with the blood of the Lord, to which he is said to have been bound and scourged," and from thence she proceeded to Bethlehem "having from her small means distributed money among the poor and her fellow-servants in Christ."[19] "Small" must be understood as a comparative term since Paula continued to dispense her bounty for the next twenty years. When she went to view the monasteries of Egypt, "she was met by the holy and venerable Bishop Isidorus the Confessor, and by innumerable crowds of monks, many of whom were exalted to the rank of priests and deacons. . . . Whose cell did she not enter? At whose feet did she not prostrate herself? Through each of these holy men she believed herself to see Christ; and whatever she bestowed on them she rejoiced that she bestowed upon the Lord. . . . Forgetful of her sex and of the weakness of her frame, she desired to dwell with her maidens among so many thousands of monks."[20] She returned to Palestine and established her residence in Bethlehem where "she remained for three years in a narrow lodging while she was building cells and monasteries and founded inns for different kinds of pilgrims by the side of the road upon which Mary and Joseph found no resting place."[21]

Paula lived in Bethlehem for seventeen more years and at one point wrote to her friend Marcella in Rome urging Marcella to join her in Bethlehem. Marcella had already become a nun, and her palace in Rome was "a kind of convent dedicated to the study of the scriptures and the psalmody and prayer."[22] Bethlehem, said Paula, was not like Rome or Jerusalem. She elaborated on this:

> In the village of Christ . . . all is rusticity, and except for psalms, silence. Withersoever you turn yourself, the ploughman, holding the plough handle, sings Alleluia; the perspiring reaper diverts himself with psalms, and the vinedresser sings some of the songs of David while he trims the vine with his curved knife. These are the ballads of this country, these are the lovesongs . . . these are whistled by the shepherds, and are the implements of the husbandman. Indeed, we do not think of what we are doing or of how we look, but see only that for which we are longing.[23]

Marcella did not come. An urban type, she undoubtedly preferred Rome to bucolic Bethlehem, and also her mentor, St. Jerome, had once admitted that "nothing is lacking to your faith, although you have not seen Jerusalem, and I am no better because I live in Bethlehem."

St. Gregory of Nyssa, once a pilgrim himself, took a dim view of pilgrimage:

> If God's grace were more plentiful in the Jerusalem area than elsewhere, then its inhabitants would not make sin so much the fashion. But as it is, there is no sort of filthy conduct they do not practice . . . cheating, adultery, theft, idolatry, poisoning, quarreling and murder are commonplace. . . . Then what proof have you in a place which allows things like that to go on, of the abundance of divine grace? . . . We knew His incarnation by the Virgin before we saw Bethlehem, we believed in His resurrection from the dead before we saw His tomb.[24]

We ourselves should pass no judgment except to recognize that the pilgrims, whoever they were, were people like those we meet every day. The Bordeaux pilgrim is the one who goes to Europe, Africa, Asia, or Disneyland and comes back to give a captive audience of friends a four-hour account of the trip illustrated with underexposed camera slides. Egeria, bless her gentle soul, would be superb at the ladies' aid. As for Paula — there are many of them!

CHAPTER III

The Enemy

Dangerous and destructive though the barbarians were, the face of barbarism was always changing. Sometimes the principal threat was from the Visigoths, sometimes from the Ostrogoths, the Vandals, or another barbarian group. The strength of these people waxed and waned. They lacked staying power; they could be fragmented; some of them actually wanted to be Romanized in their own way. They could be managed, out-witted, even defeated, and after the tacit decision was made to abandon the West, it was mainly the northern Balkan fron-tier, a much shorter line to defend, that the government at Constantinople had to guard.

On the other hand, the Romans had one civilized enemy, consistently hostile, always dangerous, and not in the least desirous of Romanization. I refer, of course, to the Persians, the Sasanian Persians.

To understand all this we have to go back a long time, far back of the "Sick Man of Europe." Most of the modern states of the Middle East have been until recently little more than pawns on the chessboards of the major powers, but it was not always so. Once it had been the other way around. Once there had been an Assyrian Empire which controlled much of the Near East and to which some peripheral Greeks paid tribute.

After that the people of the West had had to reckon with three successive Iranian powers: first, the Achaemenid Persians, then the Parthians, and finally the Sasanians. Even the Greco-Macedonian Seleucids who ruled the East in the interval between the Achaemenid and the Parthian periods had an empire more Oriental than Greek and were regarded as a Near Eastern power and often feared as such by their western neighbors.

At any rate, as the West grew in strength, the struggle of Orient and Occident became a more even contest, but the people of the West had always to be on guard. In their earliest phases all three Iranian empires were especially menacing, although each time the initial impetus of the Iranian thrust was lost partly because of dynastic quarreling, or internal disorders, or foreign pressures coming simultaneously from East and West. It was also true that as the Iranians controlled wider and wider areas outside their homeland they always faced problems of military manpower to garrison and protect their far-flung domains, and they had to keep in subjection or attempt to retain the loyalties of diverse non-Iranian peoples. Fortunately for the West, therefore, there was a limit to Oriental imperial expansion, and the fighting was mostly confined to regions that both East and West wanted to control: Anatolia, Syria, Palestine, and Egypt.

The Achaemenids and the Sasanians were truly Persian dynasties, but the Parthians were interlopers despite their claims to legitimacy and descent from the Achaemenids. The Sasanians took their name from Sasan, a priest of the mother goddess Anahita. Sasan lived near Persepolis in southwestern Iran at the beginning of the third century A.D. One of his sons, Papak, overthrew and then usurped the throne of a native ruler there in the province of Fars about 208, but he was never recognized as a legitimate vassal by the Parthian king, nor would the Parthians accept Shapur, one of Papak's sons, as his successor. For this matter, the authority of Shapur was not recognized by his own brother, Ardashir, but Shapur died before any serious fraternal strife developed between the two. Consequently, it was Ardashir who unified southwestern Persia and warred successfully against the Parthian king, Artabanus, killing him in battle in 224. By 227 Ctesiphon, the Parthian capital on the Tigris, had fallen, and Ardashir had founded the Sasanian Empire.

Ardashir, whose name is the Sasanian equivalent of Artaxerxes, reigned until 243. He managed to unify Iran, to hold Mesopotamia, and to defeat the King of Armenia in spite of Roman meddling and pressures exerted from the east by the Kushan king in Pakistan. Far from cowed by the might of Rome, the victorious Ardashir also captured some Roman garrison towns in northwestern Mesopotamia.

Before his death Ardashir associated with himself as ruler his son Shapur who as Shapur I, the second Sasanian king, reigned from 243 to 273 and was no less successful than his father. The territory of the Kushans was invaded and some of it lopped off to become Sasanian property. The Roman emperors Gordian III and Philip the Arab were less than effective against Shapur whose greatest triumph, however, was the defeat and capture of the Emperor Valerian in 259. Not far from Carrhae, the site of a comparable Roman disaster three centuries before where the Parthians had destroyed Crassus and his army (53 B.C.), Valerian was taken as the slave of Shapur. Alive, Valerian was used as a stepping stone or mounting block when Shapur wanted to mount his horse; dead, he was mounted as a trophy by an able taxidermist. The disgrace of Valerian and the Romans was complete. The soldiers of Valerian captured by Shapur were carried off and settled in Iran where their technological skills as architects and engineers were employed by the Sasanians to build roads, bridges, and irrigation dams, some of which can still be seen. It was Shapur who commemorated his victories with the famous sculptured reliefs at Bishapur and Naqsh-i-Rustam, the burial place of the Achaemenids. A founder of cities, Shapur did not neglect to advertise his success: one town was named Weh Antiok Shapur, "the better Antioch of Shapur," and another Peroz Shapur, "the Victory of Shapur."

A dozen such towns were established or refounded, and each was managed by a *shahrab*, a steward of imperial cities. Each town had an area or territorium attached to it in Seleucid or Roman fashion, the whole constituting a taxable unit. We shall speak later of another major development of Shapur's reign: his alliance with the Manichaeans.

After Shapur I two of his sons and one of his grandsons reigned in brief succession, but at last dynastic confusion brought to the throne still another of Shapur's sons, Narses (293-302), who represented the junior branch of the royal house. Narses fared poorly against Diocletian, losing not merely a battle but also his queen, his harem, and a considerable slice of territory. Nor did the son of Narses, who reigned to 309, manage to improve the family fortunes. It was the kind of respite the Romans sorely needed after what they had suffered from Ardashir and Shapur I. But Shapur II, grandson of Narses and great-grandson of the first Shapur, changed all that. During his reign of seventy years (309-79) he caused both Romans and Kushans no end of trouble, and his harsh treatment of his Christian subjects was memorable to say the least. Before we can examine in detail the exploits of the major Sasanian king, however, something needs to be said about the Sasanians in general.

The Sasanians are not well known to us, but they were obviously of great importance in the fourth century. It is not that there are no scholars or have been none who rank as specialists in Sasanian history. The difficulty is that their published works are scattered and sometimes difficult to find; there is very little in English. Herzfeld and Ghirshman are familiar names but more because of their work on the Achaemenid and earlier periods. Yet both men made spectacular discoveries in Sasanian archaeology. The basic history of the Sasanians, however, is still that of Arthur Christensen, a work in French entitled *L'Iran sous les Sassanids*; the second edition was published in Copenhagen in 1944.

The sources for the Sasanians are varied. There are works in Greek and Latin, Armenian and Syriac, as well as later histories in Arabic and Persian; there is even a brief Chinese notice dating from the seventh century. In addition to the literary materials there are inscriptions in Middle Persian (a Pahlevi dialect), trilinguals in Aramaic, Parthian (another Pahlevi dialect), and Middle Persian, and some bilinguals in the latter two. Some papyri in Middle Persian were found at Dura. Other sources which have and must be used are coins, seal impressions and seal rings, and various other objects of art: gold and silver vessels, mostly of the embossed variety, rock carvings, paintings, mosaics, and so on. As with the Parthians, numismatists have been able to use the coins to great advantage. The Sasanians issued gold *dinars* (denarii), silver *dirhems* (*drachmae*) and diobols (half drachmae) as well as silver *sters* (staters) tariffed at four dirhems each. The obverse of Sasanian coins bears the king's portrait; the reverse displays a fire altar.

It is frequently said that there were two main characteristics of Sasanian organization: they created a centralized state, as opposed to the feudal one of the Parthians, and they set up a state church. Among the Sasanians there were four estates (in the French sense). There were the ecclesiastics, the warriors, the bureaucrats, and the common people. Each estate was divided into subclasses. The ecclesiastics were priests and judges; the warriors, cavalry and foot; the bureaucrats were scribes, accountants, notaries, doctors, poets, and astrologers; and the commons were farmers, artisans, etc. Socially, there were the rulers, kings and princes headed by the *shahanshah*, King of Kings; subkings and governors; the seven great noble families; the lesser nobles; and the free men. The major officials were the grand vizier, the secretary of the treasury, commander in chief of the army, secretaries corresponding to the Roman magistri (or earlier praepositi), and in the church organization there were the magi or mobads headed by the mobad of mobads, the Zoroastrian pope.

Although the basis of the Sasanian economy was agriculture, trade and manufacturing were extremely lucrative as far as the government was concerned. The importation of raw silk from

China was a royal monopoly, and the manufacture of silks became a flourishing Sasanian industry along with the production of glass. As among the Romans of the same period, there were great estates belonging to the nobles on which a self-sufficient economy prevailed, and there was a tendency for the great nobles to become increasingly independent of the king. Ultimately, after our period, a struggle developed between the nobles and the commons in which various rulers found it to their advantage to support one side or the other; it is not surprising to discover that in the end the common people were the losers.

The state religion of the Sasanians did indeed become Zoroastrianism, but not without a struggle. The prophet and founder, Zoroaster, who had lived in the sixth century B.C., might not have recognized the Zoroastrianism of the Sasanians as having much connection with his teachings; he certainly would have rejected many Sasanian beliefs. Especially repugnant to Zoroaster would have been the alliance with his old enemies, the magi, and the polytheism of the religion which involved the worship of Anahita, the mother goddess, and Mithra, once a sky god but later identified with the sun. On the other hand, Sasanian Zoroastrianism was more typically Iranian than the faith of Zoroaster himself and more acceptable to ordinary people of the time.

The general trend among the Sasanians was thus toward a modified Zoroastrianism. Ardashir, the first king, had commanded a translation of the Avesta into Middle Persian, but his religious interests seem to have been no more important in his scheme of things than his desire for the broad modernization of Sasanian culture since he also encouraged the translation of Indian and Greek works on medicine, astronomy, and metaphysics. The coronation of Shapur I, however, coincided with the rise of the new prophet, Mani. The mother of Mani was said to have been a descendant of the Arsacids, the Parthian ruling house, and his father, originating in Median Ecbatana (Hamadan), had migrated to Babylon where Mani was born about

216. The future prophet was brought up among a sect known as the "baptizers." He was subject to visions and at last received true divine secrets from an angel. It was also said that before he began to preach, he had made a journey to India. When mature, his theology was nothing if not eclectic, a potpourri of current beliefs, drawing upon Zoroastrianism, Christianity, and Gnosticism. The only real competitor of such a catchall was Christianity.

In the beginning, said Mani, there were two opposites: Light and Darkness. The former represented the spirit or soul of man and the latter, his body. The ultimate goal was the emancipation of soul from body as in Greek philosophy and the Gnostic beliefs. Baptism, communion, and absolution were Manichaean rites, and there was a Holy Trinity composed of the Father of Grandeur, Primitive Man, and the Mother of Living. Associated with the father of Grandeur were five houses or attributes: intelligence, reason, thought, reflection, and will. The rival of the Father was the King of Darkness associated with fire, wind, water, clouds, and smoke. Despite its obvious indebtedness to some phases of Judaism, that religion was disavowed by the Manichaeans. Moses and the prophets were branded as devils, and Jesus and Buddha were called true prophets and precursors of Mani. Just as the Achaemenid, Darius the Great, had been a convert of Zoroaster's, so Shapur I became a Manichaean, and Zoroastrianism lost ground. After Shapur's death, however, a reaction set in. Mani was declared a heretic by the magi. He was imprisoned, tortured, and finally died in 276.

The new Sasanian king, Vahram II (276-93), was supported and guided by a priest named Kartir, the governor of the temple of Anahita, who rose to the post of soul keeper of the King of Kings. Under Kartir's influence Vahram made Zoroastrianism the state religion, introduced a new iconography extremely visible in Persian art, and persecuted Manichaeans, Christians, and Buddhists.

The wind veered again during the dynastic quarrels that brought Narses to the throne in 293. Narses championed Manichaeanism and so gained allies among the Arabs and the Egyptians to whom the religion had now spread. The Manichaeans, and thus the Sasanians, were blamed by Diocletian for the Egyptian revolt of Domitianus which coincided with the Persian War of 297, and several years before Diocletian's great persecution of the Christians the Manichaeans were his principal target. In his edict of 296, transmitted to the Roman proconsul of Africa by Diocletian, confiscation of property and the death penalty were prescribed for Manichaean leaders, and Roman officials who had adopted Manichaeanism were to be sent to the mines as slaves. Manichaean religious texts were to be burned. Diocletian deplored the spread of new beliefs that might undermine ancient paganism. He said in part:

> We take note that . . . the Manichaeans have set up new and unheard-of sects in opposition to the older creeds, with the intent of driving out to the benefit of their depraved doctrine what was formerly granted to us by divine favor. We have heard that these men have but recently sprung up and advanced, like strange and unexpected portents, from the Persian people, our enemy, to this part of the world, where they are perpetrating many outrages, disturbing the tranquillity of the peoples and also introducing the gravest harm to the communities. And it is to be feared that . . . they may try, with the accursed customs and perverse laws of the Persians, to infect men of a more innocent nature, namely the temperate and tranquil Roman people, as well as our entire Empire with what one might call their malevolent poisons.[1]

With the accession of Shapur II in 309, however, Zoroastrianism staged a victorious comeback in Persia. In time it was employed by that ruler as a counter to Christianity which was on its way to becoming a virtual state religion of the Romans. Shapur, like Constantine, found an alliance with a religious sect advantageous—another reminder of the power and importance of religious groups in the fourth century.

As a footnote, it is worth observing that in addition to the sacred books of the Zoroastrians and various Christian commentaries, our principal sources for the religious developments just described are inscriptions: those of Narses and Vahram II pieced together by Herzfeld and the materials found by Ghirsh-man at Bishapur.[2] There are also paintings in caves depicting the Manichaeans.[3]

⬦⬦⬦⬦⬦⬦⬦⬦⬦⬦⬦⬦⬦⬦

The fortunes of the Sasanians were at a low ebb at the be-ginning of the fourth century, but, as we have said, a new era was about to dawn. Under Shapur II the Sasanians would rise to new heights once the young king attained his majority and Constantine the Great had passed from the scene. For a long time after 309, however, Shapur was a mere child, not ready to govern, so that affairs were managed by a regency composed of the queen mother and the nobles. The deeds of the mature Shapur were sufficient to establish his reputation for greatness, and they also provided the foundations on which the Shapur of legend was to be built. In later times there were endless stories about him not only as a grown man but also as a pre-cocious child. As an example of the former, he was given in legend the nickname "Crusher of Shoulders;" there were vari-ous stories about his treatment of captives who were rendered unfit for further warfare by having their shoulders broken or pierced. Actually, this seems to have arisen from a misunder-standing about one of his titles which signified "one who bears a weight of responsibility on his shoulders." As a child it was re-lated that he showed great perception and alertness. On one oc-casion at Ctesiphon he was awakened by a great noise. When he inquired about its source, he was told it was caused by throngs of people struggling to cross the Tigris on a single bridge: some were trying to cross it to enter the city and others were going in the opposite direction attempting to leave town. Shapur solved the problem immediately by ordering that a second bridge should be constructed so that the traffic going in one direction could use the first bridge and that proceeding in the other direction could use the second. One is compelled to wonder whether this may not have been the origin of the one-way street.

The real Shapur had problems far more serious than the traffic in Ctesiphon. These were not confined to his reign but were problems for most Sasanian kings. First, there was the matter of the eastern frontier where the danger from the Kushans was complicated by the rise of the Chionite-Ephthalite kingdom which had gained its independence from the Kushans. Both the Kushans and Chionite-Ephthalites were Asiatic groups. The latter were perhaps related to the Huns, and the Kushans, who had appeared as a power as early as the first century A.D., had been part of the Yu Chi confederacy, disruptive invaders of western India in Hellenistic times. The Kushans not only threatened the Sasanians as potential invaders, but they also controlled the silk route. By pushing the Kushans out of Turkestan, Shapur got hold of Balkh, a terminus for the silk route, and by defeating the Chionite-Ephthalites he minimized the danger of an invasion from the east; some of these warlike people even became his confederates and were used in western campaigns against the Romans.

Shapur's second problem, of course, involved his frontier with Rome. He warred successfully against Constantius and Julian. In a brilliant operation in 359 he managed the capture of Amida in extreme northwestern Mesopotamia, an event described in a famous passage in Ammianus.[4] In 363 Julian's penetration to Ctesiphon was blunted as the approach of Shapur forced the Roman emperor to withdraw and move up the Tigris in a vain attempt to link up with Armenian allies coming down from the north.

Thus, Shapur's second problem was closely bound up with his third: the problem of Armenia. That country had always been a bone of contention between the Romans and whatever foe they faced in the East, Parthian or Persian. Both sides wanted to control Armenia: for the Romans it could be an open door to the invasion of Mesopotamia from the north, and for the Parthians or Sasanians it was a buffer against such an invasion. Consequently, over the centuries Armenia had been under the control, direct, sometimes indirect, of either East or West.

Following Julian's death Armenia was annexed by Shapur as a client kingdom. After Shapur it was partitioned by Rome and the Sasanians, the latter retaining control of about four-fifths of the region. Still later at the end of the fourth century as the Huns threatened the Caucasus, the Romans and Sasanians agreed on the mutual defense of the northern passes, the Romans financing works of fortification to be manned by Sasanian garrisons.

Finally, the Armenian question leads us into the fourth Sasanian problem, that of religion. Within the Sasanian realm, as we have seen, were warring factions: the Manichaeans, the Zoroastrians, and the heretical sects that had split off from whatever was defined as orthodox Zoroastrianism—a fragmentation had occurred among the Zoroastrians similar to that among the Christians. Outside the Sasanian empire, the Romans to the west were Christians and the Kushans to the east, Buddhists. Therefore, it behooved the Sasanians to take some sort of stand. They had wavered between Manichaeanism and Zoroastrianism, but Shapur chose the latter and sought to define orthodoxy by establishing the canon of the Avesta. We have previously noted parallel developments in Christianity and Judaism.

We shall deal with the Sasanian Avesta in a moment, but first it should be pointed out that the Zoroastrianism of Shapur spelled persecution for the Christians among his subjects, especially those numerous Christians in Armenia. The Armenian Christian problem continued to be troublesome after the time of Shapur, with the policies of the Sasanians shifting back and forth from harsh to lenient until the fifth century when a separate Iranian Church was established, independent of Constantinople.

To return to Shapur and orthodoxy, Shapur commanded the Grand Mobad, the Zoroastrian pope, to establish the text of the Avesta. That worthy arranged the sacred book into twenty-one Nasks or sections, and he demonstrated the authenticity of his labors by undergoing the ordeal by fire in which molten metal was poured on his chest. Little of the Sasanian Avesta has survived, but it was more than a compilation of theology because it is known that it contained encyclopedic data on science, law, morality, and legend. Moreover, by this period Ahuramazda, the god of Zoroaster, had been deprived of his unique position and relegated to membership in a pantheon that included Anahita and Mithra.

༺༺༺༺༺༺༺༺༺༺༺༺༺

Thanks mainly to Ammianus, Shapur II possesses a historical personality in contrast to other early Sasanian kings who are shadowy figures indeed. He is described as tall, a head taller than most Persians; brave, never shirking danger in warfare; easily aroused to anger, yet chivalrous and thoughtful on occasion. A good strategist and a strict disciplinarian, he was no less deficient in statecraft.

About 356, during the reign of Constantius, the Romans heard that Shapur was hard-pressed by the Chionites on his eastern frontiers, and they judged that he might be induced to make some kind of peace with Rome that would involve favorable concessions to Constantius simply to avoid having to fight on two fronts at the same time. Naturally, Constantius did not wish Shapur to know that he had troubles of his own on the Rhine and Danube frontiers and was not eager to fight in the Near East either. By the time the Roman peace feeler got to Shapur, however, the Sasanian king had vanquished his foes and interpreted the Roman overtures as a sign of weakness on their part. Therefore, he dispatched a haughty message to Constantius (paraphrased in Ammianus XVII, 5, 3-8) in which he demanded the surrender of Roman territory as far west as Macedonia and, more concretely, promised to invade and annex Armenia if Constantius did not capitulate at once. In reply, Constantius took an equally hard line, but he had not abandoned hope of a treaty and consequently sent an embassy to Shapur almost immediately. At best, this might gain a little time and allow the Romans to prepare for a new war. The embassy consisted of a count, a high-ranking secretary, and a philosopher named Eustathius who was said to be a master of persuasion. Bearing letters and gifts from Constantius, the ambassadors set off to find Shapur at Ctesiphon. The negotiations dragged on for a long time and came to nothing because neither side would make any concessions. In addition to the story as told by Ammianus, a somewhat fuller version is given by Eunapius in his *Lives of the Philosophers*:

> With regard to Eustathius, it would be sacreligious to leave out what would convey the truth. All men were agreed that he was not only observed to be a most noble character, but also most gifted with eloquence when put to the test, while the charm that sat on his tongue and lips seemed to be nothing less than witchcraft. His mildness and amiability so blossomed out in what he said and gushed forth with his words that those who heard his voice surrendered themselves like men who had tasted the lotus, and they hung on that voice and those speeches. So closely did he resemble the musical Sirens that the emperor (Constantius) for all that he was wrapped up in the books of the Christians sent for him.[5]

Eustathius was put in charge of the embassy, and the philosopher (according to Eunapius) so charmed Shapur as to leave that "tyrant a captive to his eloquence." More than that, Eustathius very nearly persuaded the Sasanian king to renounce his throne and assume the cloak and habits of a philosopher, but the forces of evil won out in the end: the magi worked hard and were finally successful in convincing Shapur that Eustathius was nothing more than a conjuror. This, then, was the reason for the failure of the embassy. A pretty story which must have pleased the orators and "philosophers" of the Fourth Century!

Eustathius, incidentally, later married the famous Sosipatra whose mind "was not like that of a woman's." Sosipatra was to eclipse her husband as a philosopher. After his death she set up a school in Pergamum where she competed successfully with the noted teacher Aedesius, a disciple of the even more famous, or notorious, Iamblichus.

Coming back to Shapur and Ammianus, when Constantius and Shapur went to war in 359 after the failure of the embassy, Ammianus was present at the siege of Amida and narrowly escaped with his life when the town fell. It was on this occasion that the historian was able to observe Shapur at first hand. One has only to read the story to learn that Ammianus was suitably impressed.

As far as the Sasanians themselves are concerned, it is unfortunate that Ammianus is less informative about them than about Shapur. He does provide a description of these Iranians, but the difficulty is that he feels, as he often does, that he must display his learning—in this case partly derived from a hasty reading of Herodotus. He does say, however:

They are almost all slender, somewhat dark, or of a leaden pallor, with eyes grim as goats, eyebrows joined and curved in the form of a half-circle, not uncomely beards, and long shaggy hair. All of them without exception even at banquets and on festal days appear girt with swords.
. . . Each man according to his means contracts many or few marriages.
. . . They avoid as they would the plague splendid and luxurious banquets and especially excessive drinking. They are immensely moderate and cautious, so much so that they sometimes march through an enemy's gardens and vineyards without touching or coveting anything, through fear of poison or magic arts. . . . On the other hand, they are so free and easy, and stroll about with such a loose and unsteady gait, that one might think them effeminate; but, in fact, they are most gallant warriors, though rather crafty than courageous, and to be feared only at long range. They are given to empty words, and talk madly and extravagantly. They are boastful, harsh and offensive, threatening in adversity and prosperity alike, crafty, haughty, cruel, claiming the power of life and death over slaves and commons. They flay men alive, either bit by bit or all at once.
. . . They stand in special fear of the laws. . . . For the office of judge, upright men of proved experience are chosen, who have little need of advice from others; therefore they ridicule our custom, which at times places eloquent men, highly skilled in public law, behind the backs of judges without learning. But that one judge is forced to take his seat on the skin of another who has been condemned to death for injustice is either a fiction of antiquity, or, if once customary, has long since been

given up. Through military training and discipline . . . they cause dread even to great armies. . . . And this nation, so bold and well trained for the dust of Mars, would have brought many other peoples under the yoke in addition to those whom they fully subdued, were they not constantly plagued by domestic wars.[6]

Ammianus did not always get everything straight, but on one occasion he was right on target. When he accompanied Julian to Ctesiphon, he saw "a pleasant and shady dwelling displaying in every part of the house after the custom of that nation, paintings representing the king killing wild beasts in various ways; for nothing in their country is painted or sculptured except slaughter in divers forms and scenes of war."[7]

We have many examples of Sasanian art—silks, sculptured reliefs, handsome embossed metal work, beautiful gems—and it is true that the favorite motifs are those of warfare and hunting. Virtually the only exceptions are sculptured scenes of the investiture of kings and the representations of deities, often of the goddess Anahita. Two things are especially noteworthy: first, the Sasanian scenes of warfare and the chase are well within the Iranian tradition; they begin with the Achaemenids and run through Parthian and Sasanian art and into the magnificent miniatures of medieval Persia. Second, Sasanian art influenced the Byzantines and the people of the medieval West. We can see this clearly in symbols and motifs. As for other cultural borrowings, it will be recalled that Manichaeanism was the root of certain Christian heresies not the least of which was the Albigensian movement in southern France that sparked a bloody crusade in the thirteenth century.

So this was the enemy. We shall encounter him again when we come to Libanius and Julian the Apostate.

CHAPTER IV

The Orator
and the Emperor

As we all know, every city has a character or personality of its own. St. Paul and Minneapolis are noticeably and defiantly different; New York is not like San Francisco; Chicago is the opposite of Boston; and Washington, in spite of everything, is a unique and beautiful place. And so it was in the ancient world. Rome, Alexandria, Athens, and the parvenu Constantinople were all different. Distinct from all others, too, was Antioch, the Fair Crown of the Orient.

Antioch on the Orontes, Antioch in Syria, founded in 300 B.C. by Seleucus I, Roman from 64 B.C., captured by the Arabs in A.D. 637, was more or less controlled by the Romans for 700 years. I say more or less because Antioch was notorious for its riotous, impudent populace. Urban populations were riotous everywhere—Rome, Alexandria, Constantinople—in a variety of ways. Rome had a howling, headless mob; Alexandria was violent, seething, ready for a lynching at the slightest provocation; the people of Constantinople often behaved like an excited Italian or Argentine crowd after a soccer match; but the people of Antioch were exceptional in that they had a sense of humor—nothing gentle, to be sure, but characterized by a biting sarcasm that found chinks even in the armored self-esteem of sophists and emperors.

Antioch was the administrative center of Rome in the Near East, the bastion of defense first against the Parthians and then against the Sasanians. In the Roman imperial period three legions were stationed there, and there was a fleet based at Antioch's port Seleucia Pieria. Antioch had other distinctions. It was famous for its school of sculpture, and it was known for its orators. Libanius, one of the principals selected for discussion in this chapter, was perhaps the greatest of Antioch's orators, closely followed by his pupil John Chrysostom, who became Patriarch at Constantinople in 397.

Like other great cities of the Roman Empire, Antioch had a large Jewish community. It was a natural target for the first Christian missionaries and it will be recalled that Barnabas and St. Paul were active there. By the beginning of the second century A.D. Antioch had a sizable Christian population. It was the see of Bishop Ignatius, famous for his letters written to the churches of Asia as he was being led off to Rome to be thrown to wild animals in the Coliseum. That was 115 A.D., the year of the great earthquake at Antioch when the Emperor Trajan narrowly escaped death as the building in which he was sleeping collapsed. In the official version of the incident Trajan was led to safety by a personage of greater than human stature, presumably Jupiter Optimus Maximus. The Christians were blamed for the earthquake, and Ignatius, who had been less than polite to Trajan, was singled out for punishment.

Located at the eastern end of the Amuk plain, about fifteen miles from the Mediterranean, Antioch was served by its port Seleucia Pieria, and the Orontes River as far as Antioch, like the Tiber up to Rome, could be navigated from the sea to the city. Although the Amuk region farther up the Orontes was a swamp swarming with mosquitoes, Antioch was protected from insect pests and heat in summer by a reliable wind from the sea that blew up the river through a funnel formed by the mountains. The mountains also determined the general layout of the city: its major axis lay along the river, and its breadth was severely limited by Mt. Silpius and associated hills. Down river toward the sea was the famous Mt. Casius, the Olympus of the gods of Ugarit in an earlier age and sacred to Zeus in the Greco-Roman period. With a salubrious climate, adequate rainfall, and good soil the region was agriculturally productive so that in normal times the city could be fed by the surrounding countryside. Sometimes, however, there was famine; and there were earthquakes, too frequent for comfort; and there were floods, mostly in winter when a stream draining off Silpius and Mt. Staurin poured a torrent down into the Orontes. This Donkey-Drowner, as it was called, was ultimately tamed by a dam known as the Iron Gate.

One of the features of Antioch was the island in the river on which were located the Circus (a race course), Diocletian's palace, and the Golden House of Constantine, an octagonal church with a gilded roof begun by Constantine and dedicated by Constantius in 341. South of Antioch about five miles away was the suburb of Daphne with its many villas and the famous temple and grove of Apollo. We have from the fourth century a marvelous mosaic which portrays in succession the principal buildings and monuments of the city: the main street, the bridge across the Orontes linking the mainland and the island, the octagonal church and the Circus, the shops in town, the road to Daphne lined with villas, a martyrion, and the Olympic stadium.

The Olympic Games at Antioch had a long and chequered history. Founded by Augustus, they were altertately suppressed and revived by his successors until finally established on a permanent basis late in the second century. The games occurred at five-year intervals, and in such "Olympic years" they consumed some forty-five days in the months of July and August. There was something for everyone: running, wrestling, poetry and rhetorical contests.

In addition to the Olympic games there were the annual games staged under the auspices of the provincial assembly of Syria. These were the responsibility of the Syriarch, usually a member of the council of Antioch who undertook this task as a liturgy. Wild beast hunts and gladiatorial shows were long the standard fare, although the latter were suppressed by Constantine in 325. Other liturgies involved putting on chariot races, the most expensive of which came at New Years' when gold was expected to be thrown to the populace.

Other entertainment was provided by theatrical shows, mostly mimes, produced by guilds of performers. An interesting feature of the Antiochene theater was the claque employed to applaud the performers, both actors and dancers. Consisting of 400 persons, the claque was used to give an illusion of popular support for certain local officials. Even bishops hired the group to applaud sermons or statements involving a doctrinal position. In a negative way the claque constituted an instrument for chastening unpopular governors. By withholding applause and greeting the end of the official's speech with a dead silence the message of disapproval was delivered more effectively than with jeers and catcalls. To have one's high-flown rhetoric plummet to earth with a dull and sickening thud must have been disheartening to say the least.

An extreme example of the operation of the claque is to be found in the famous "Riot of the Statues" that occured in 387. After the military disaster at Adrianople in 378, army reorganization and rebuilding brought sharply increased taxes. Protest riots took place in many cities of the eastern half of the empire, and one of the most severe was at Antioch. The first part of the story, at least, has a familiar ring:

In hope of moderating the imperial demands for funds, the councillors and many prominent citizens of Antioch went in a body to the governor. Failing to get any satisfaction from him, they called on the local bishop, who just happened to be out of town. At this point a milling crowd had gathered and was spurred into action by the theatrical claque, directed, as it turned out, by a notorious agitator who had come up from Beyrut for the purpose. After shouting itself hoarse, the crowd became a frenzied mob that first tried to break into the residence of the governor, then rushed into a nearby public bath, crashed about and mischievously cut all the ropes supporting the lamps that illuminated the building. Next, painted panels bearing the imperial portraits were smashed to bits and the bronze statues of Theodosius, his empress, and his son Arcadius were overturned. Finally, the crowd stormed and set fire to the house of a prominent citizen who was believed to be in favor of the new taxes.

The authorities, the Count of the East and the guard, now moved in. Alleged ringleaders were arrested and executed: some were beheaded, some burned alive, and others thrown to wild beasts. The entire council was penned up and threatened with extermination, but the homilies of St. John Chrysostom, the intervention of holy monks who came down from the hills, the return of the bishop, and the strong protests of the leading pagan orator as well as the realization by the imperial authorities that they had gone too far at last produced a relaxation in the government attitude and the release of the councillors.

The pagan orator was Libanius (314-93), one of the most important people in Antioch in the fourth century and certainly the one we know best. Very much in addition to a biographical notice in Eunapius' *Lives of the Philosophers*, we have sixty-four of Libanius' orations and 1,540 of his letters. A real anachronism, Libanius was neither a sophist nor a philosopher, but an orator. He was considered an outsider by the sophist clique because he had never had sophistic training and because even at Athens he had not had a first-class teacher. Nevertheless, without being a member of the club, Libanius exercised more influence in Antioch and Constantinople than his jealous rivals.

Libanius is important for our purposes not because he was a major literary figure or because he was one of the powers in Antioch or because of his intimacy with the Emperor Julian and other famous people, but rather because he has left us an autobiography. The *Oratio I* is far more useful to us than a mere biography since the subject is speaking of himself rather than being spoken about, and he is dealing with what to him is the most interesting topic in the world. What he has to say reveals to us Libanius as a person, an individual, and a representative of a group—the pagan intellectuals of the East. In this sense he is the Oriental counterpart of Symmachus at Rome. Furthermore, his testimony and his attitudes reinforce certain impressions of the essence of the Fourth Century that we have already received from the Theodosian Code and will derive from other sources as we go along.

Libanius belonged to a prominent family long active in the civic life of Antioch. On both his father's and his mother's side of the family were ancestors and relatives who had held important municipal offices. There was a rumor that his *epipappos* (great-grandfather) had come from Italy, but this seems to have been based on the fact that the old fellow had known Latin, a rarity in the East, and had once composed a speech in that language. What was more important to Libanius himself was that his ancestor had possessed the power of divination and had foreseen the ruin of his progeny. Libanius' father had died early, and the orator and his two brothers were brought up by their mother who very wisely withdrew from the city into the country for that purpose. This rural childhood was the happiest period of Libanius' unhappy life, for there he enjoyed a normal sort of boyhood. He loved his pigeons, had the usual passionate interest in sports, the chariot races, and the theater, although he was not so high on gladiatorial spectacles. Looking ahead to the future, he spurned the conventional careers in local politics, the law, or even, he says, imperial administration, and instead plunged into a study of the classics. As Marcus Aurelius would have said, "he did not fall into the hands of any sophist," although in reality this was more by accident than design. The fact was that the only respectable teacher in Antioch was an old-line professor of literature, but the advantages of this became obvious to Libanius later: he could speak and write well because he could draw on models from Homer to Menander and was not forced to use the patois of his age, just as today he would not have had to rely on the "in" words of the moment or ape the jargon of television newscasters. His writings reveal his acquaintance with Homer, Hesiod, Pindar, and the Athenian dramatists, Aesop, Demosthenes, Isocrates, and, for better or worse, the Asianic orator Aristides.

At twenty Libanius was struck by lightning and completely discombobulated. Understandingly, this was a trauma. He was henceforth plagued by awful nightmares and subject to migraine which he also blamed on his accident. He was always ailing. In later life he was the victim of the gout, a common discomfort of the Roman period. Like his hero, the orator Aristides, Libanius enjoyed poor health and apparently enjoyed even more telling everybody about it. Nervous, delicate, paranoid, and self-centered, he could be infinitely tiresome.

At twenty-two or so, near the end of Constantine's reign, Libanius set off for Athens to pursue advanced studies just as Julian, St. Basil, St. Gregory, and others would do later. He traveled by public post to Constantinople and then by ship to Athens, ailing all the way. On arriving in Athens, he was kidnapped by the students of a certian mediocre teacher named Diophantus who had nothing to teach that Libanius did not already know. Eunapius sneers that, as the pupil of Diophantus, Libanius did not have to run the risk of being obscured by his fellow students and teachers, but Libanius had a different version:

> I had heard tales of fighting between the schools which took place in the heart of Athens: I had heard of the cudgels, the knives and stones they used and the wounds they inflicted, of the resultant court actions, the pleas of the defence and the verdicts upon the guilty, and of all those deeds of derring-do which students perform to raise the prestige of their teachers. I used to think them noble in their hardihood and no less justified than those who took up arms for their country: I used to pray heaven that it should be my lot too to distinguish myself so, to go hotfoot to the Peiraeus or Sunium or other ports to kidnap students at their landing, and then go . . . to Corinth to stand trial for kidnapping, give a string of parties, run through all I had, and then look for someone to make me a loan. But fortune knew that I would be heading for ruin in this specious trap with its high sounding title of "head of the school,"

and so . . . she withdrew me from the teacher whom I used to regard as the proper recipient of such services on my part, and took me off to be the pupil of someone else, under whom I would become acquainted only with the labours connected with rhetoric.[1]

Libanius goes on to say that because he had been kidnapped and dragged unwillingly to the inferior school, his classmates hesitated to compel him to engage in wild escapades. Instead, he studied hard and refused even to play ball (literally) or to have anything to do with the singing girls "who have wrecked the career of many a man." In the end, too, he came to realize that the students of the famous teacher with whom he had intended to enroll were generally undistinguished and that his kidnapping was a blessing in disguise.

After four years—he had planned to stay eight—Libanius left Athens and taught successfully at Constantinople until a jealous rival accused him of having resorted to an astrologer, all this based on evidence provided under torture by a scribe snatched from the entourage of Libanius. After a short sojourn at Nicaea, he was invited to teach at Nicomedia where he enjoyed great popularity that made him a target for rivals who were losing students. Once again Libanius was accused of practicing magic, this time to bring about the death of a rival professor's wife. Ultimately, refusing posts at both Athens and Constantinople, Libanius returned to his native city of Antioch to become its principal orator and teacher and to engage in the practice of law. Under the tyranny of the Caesar Gallus he nearly lost his life when it was alleged that he had cut off the heads of two young girls and used them for brewing magic that was intended to harm both Gallus and Constantius.

This will give you an idea of the *Oratio I*. It is full of tales of fantastic success, plots of competitors, illness, hard luck, etc., etc. Deaths in the family caused Libanius' hair to turn white; he came down with the gout; his nightmares returned. He got agoraphobia. "I avoided the center of the city. I feared the great baths and every house but my own. A cloud would descend upon my eyes, bouts of dizziness would overcome me."[2] Then Asclepius vouched him three visions, two of which came in the daytime, and he was temporarily cured.

After this came the trials under Valens, including the episode of the ouija board. Libanius was nearly caught in the imperial net: he had consulted a soothsayer about his headaches and nearly lost his head in consequence. He had also had some dealings with a man who practiced divination from birds, and there was a letter of Libanius' to prove it. It was a narrow escape!

Other calamities followed. His brother died; his beloved mother had died earlier. His illness returned and the gout as well. Of his students the best ones had all died without proving their worth, and people were sneering that Libanius had never turned out a distinguished product. Some of you may recognize all this as an antique version of the familiar question, "How many graduate students does he or she have?"

The friends of Libanius persuaded him that his illness was caused by some enemy invoking magic against him. They told him he ought to sue somebody, but he had so many enemies it was hard to pick a target. His friends were proved right in the end: a dead chameleon was found hidden in the classroom, and, after it was disposed of, Libanius began to recover.

Other misfortunes came in a flood. His common-law wife died, "the woman who was the mother of my son and better than any servant." His son was injured in an accident. He began to lose students as the more ambitious deserted the study of Greek for that of Latin so that they could learn Roman law or get into the bureaucracy. Libanius himself knew no Latin and had no intention of improving himself in that regard. It is a sad story, and Libanius pulls out all the stops. As Livy said of Cicero, "he bore none of his misfortunes as a man should."

Perhaps the greatest triumph of Libanius, certainly the greatest as far as Libanius himself was concerned, was his brief intimacy with the Emperor Julian the Apostate. Julian was in every way pleasing to Libanius. He seemed about to set the world at rights by restoring paganism; he was so enamored of Greek that

his Latin style was notoriously poor; best of all, Julian professed to be absolutely overwhelmed by the great oratorical
talents of Libanius. We shall talk about the meeting of the emperor and the orator presently, but first a few things should
be said about Julian.

Flavius Claudius Julianus was born at Constantinople in 331.
His father was Julius Constantius, a half-brother of Constantine
the Great. Twice married, Julius was also the father of the
probably deservedly ill-fated Caesar Gallus by his first wife;
his second wife, Basilina, presented him with Julian. At six
Julian was already an orphan; his mother died early, and his
father was eliminated by the sons of Constantine, his own
nephews, as they cleared from the board possible claimants
for the throne. Afterward, not satisfied with this, they began
to gobble up one another until by 350 only Constantius II was
left. All this time the lives of Julian and Gallus hung by a thread,
and for Gallus the thread was severed in 354 after he had failed
as a Caesar to please his uncle and practically everyone else.

On the other hand, Julian, while closely watched, had escaped the purge because he was so quiet and studious, coopera-
tive, and unobtrusive. But the still water ran deeper than anyone suspected. Ostensibly a devout Catholic—that is, if anyone
raised in the Arian faith could be so regarded—Julian had secretly reverted to paganism before his twentieth birthday when
he began a round of advanced studies at Pergamum, Ephesus,
and finally at Athens where he covertly got himself initiated
into the Eleusinian mysteries. By this time also Julian had not
found complete satisfaction in rhetorical or philosophical
studies. Instead, philosophy had led him off to the periphery
of Neo-Platonism into the domain of the masters of divination
and magical hocus-pocus. Such wonder workers could produce
results, immediate and far more spectacular, than any derived
from disciplined ratiocination. The Great Thurston of this
group was Maximus of Ephesus who possessed a nimble tongue
and even quicker hands which made him a master of prestidigi-
tation. Overwhelmed by the apparent wisdom of Maximus,

Julian became his devoted follower. Julian would have been even more impressed had he known that Maximus foresaw his (Julian's) untimely end and later was to predict what would happen to Valens at Adrianople. Julian and Libanius thus shared a positive and unshakable belief in magic and divination, but they were not alone in this as the Theodosian code bears witness.

Gallus died in 354. Constantius had no son and finally turned for a successor to Julian, the last of the line of Constantius Chlorus. Invested as Caesar in Milan in 355, Julian was married to Helena, the spinster sister of Constantius. Whether this unhappy couple were incompatible or whether, as it was said, the Empress Eusebia was determined that Helena should not bear a child, there were no children of this marriage. Moreover, Helena died within a few years.

At any rate, the new Caesar was assigned to Gaul, overrun by barbarians from across the Rhine, while Constantius hurried back to the East to deal with our old friend Shapur II. In Gaul the meek, retiring, little scholar suddenly blossomed into a soldier and a leader of men. He defeated the Alamanni and the Franks, four times crossed the Rhine into Germany, wrote Gallic Commentaries in the style of Julius Caesar (but in Greek), and won the hearts of the people of Gaul by reducing taxes and keeping a tight rein on the bureaucrats. The military success and growing popularity of Julian were just as displeasing to Constantius as the failures and unpopularity of Gallus. Claiming that he needed reinforcements in the East, Constantius ordered the transfer of a large contingent of Julian's forces to the Orient. Neither the prospect of a change of climate nor the idea of fighting Persians appealed to Julian's veterans. They mutinied and proclaimed Julian their Augustus. His choices were then immediate death at the hands of his own men or rebellion and very probable execution at the hands of Constantius if he failed to overcome that experienced commander. But his luck held. Constantius died in Cilicia in 361 before there was any test of strength and skill, and Julian became emperor unopposed.

An enigma to us and to most of his contemporaries, fair game for modern novelists, we can never know Julian any better than we know Alexander the Great or Julius Caesar or any other controversial and legendary figure. Hero or anti-Christ, philosopher or half-baked scholar, we cannot opt for any extreme. He could be charming; he could be dull; he could be brilliant and witty; he could be crude, utterly lacking in taste as in the *Misopogon*. Mortal, credulous, the victim of a sophistic education and a divided culture, Julian deserves more pity than censure.

Julian comes off best in some of his letters — if, indeed, they *are* his. Near the end of 361 he wrote as follows to his uncle Julian, his mother's brother, later Count of the East at Antioch:

> The third hour of the night has just begun, and as I have no secretary to dictate to because they are all occupied, I have with difficulty made the effort to write this to you myself. I am alive, by the grace of the gods, and have been freed from the necessity of either suffering or inflicting irreparable ill. But the Sun . . . and sovereign Zeus also bear me witness that never for a moment did I wish to slay Constantius, but rather I wished the contrary. Why then did I come . . . because the gods expressly ordered me and promised me safety . . . furthermore I came because having been declared a public enemy I meant to frighten him merely and that our quarrel should result in intercourse and more friendly terms, but if we should have to decide the issue by battle, I meant to entrust the whole to fortune and the gods, and so await whatever their clemency might decide.[3]

As an example of Julian's charm and simplicity, we might quote a portion of a letter presenting a tiny farm to the rhetorician Evagrius:

> This property is not more than two and a half miles from the sea; it is not, therefore, pestered with people selling things, nor with sailors and their tiresome chatter; on the other hand it is not devoid of the gifts of Nereus, for you get fresh fish there, so fresh that it is acutally gasping, and if you leave the house and mount a little rise, you will see the Prepontis with its islands, and the city named after the great Emperor (Constantinople). Then you need not walk on seaweed or slime, nor are you

incommoded by the unpleasing and nameless refuse which the sea casts up upon the sands; you tread on herbs and thyme, and sweet-smelling turf. There is peace profound on the place, whether you want to lie at ease with a book, or to rest your eyes by gazing on the loveliest of sights, the sea with its ships. When I was a youngster I thought this the most delightful of summer retreats, for there is plenty of running water, and a charming bath, a garden and trees. When I grew up I used to long for it, and often went there, and my visits there were never without literary occupation.[4]

That Julian had a good sense of humor is suggested by an exchange of letters between him and Eustathius, the unsuccessful envoy of Constantius to Shapur II whom we have already met. Julian, mindful of the comfort of his friend, had given him the special privilege of making a journey via the imperial post. Eustathius replied:

What good luck that the permit to travel by Imperial post arrived too late! Instead of shaking with fright, perched on the post carriage, being jolted on to the drunken muleteers, and the mules . . . fat with laziness and over-eating, enduring clouds of dust, and the barbarous shoutings of the drivers and cracking of whips, I can travel at leisure, along a covered, shady road, well provided with springs and halting-places for the hour of repose. So I have a fragrant rest under the shade of spreading planes or cypresses, with my *Phaedrus* or other book of Plato in my hand. Enjoying this untrammelled mode of travel, O divine and sacred master, I thought it unnatural not to write and tell you about it.[5]

Julian could be brusque and unkind. To the "uneducated Cynics" he quoted the proverb, "Much learning does not teach men to have understanding," and he also said, "When you imitate one of those early Cynics by carrying a staff and wearing your hair long, do you think that you gain a reputation with the crowd? One or two used to applaud Diogenes in his own day, but more than ten times ten thousand had their stomachs turned by nausea and loathing." In the *Caesars* Julian was harshly critical of Augustus and less than polite to Constantine. In that contest for excellence, it was not surprising that Julian passed over even Alexander the Great and Julius Caesar to award the prize to Marcus Aurelius, his ideal.

Still another aspect of Julian's character emerges in connection with his concern for the books of George, the unsavory bishop murdered by a mob in Alexandria. He commanded that the library collected by George be found and sent to Antioch. In the collection there were works on philosophy and rhetoric, and also "on the teachings of the impious Galilaeans." As Julian admitted, "Some men have a passion for horses, others for birds, others, again, for wild beasts; but I, from childhood, have been penetrated by a passionate longing to acquire books."[6]

After winning the throne, Julian came to Constantinople at the end of 361 to embark on an ambitious program of reform. He first cleaned house by getting rid of the associates of Constantius, reducing the size of the staff at court, and suppressing the hated secret service. Then he proclaimed freedom of worship: pagans and Christians alike could worship as they pleased, and the orthodox clergy persecuted and exiled by the Arian Constantius were recalled. The pagan temples despoiled by the Christians were to be restored and services resumed. Julian's leniency did not divide the Christians as he had hoped. Instead, he was forced to take a harder and harder line against all Christians as he sought to establish a kind of universal pagan church.

Many of the stricter measures were enacted by Julian at Antioch where he came in 362 to prepare for the war against Shapur II. The decrees dismissing Christians from teaching positions financed by state funds, prohibiting them from using the public post, and the attacks and ridicule launched by the emperor himself upon the Galilaeans did not make his situation in Antioch any more comfortable, compounded as it was by a local crop failure, a wheat shortage aggravated by the presence of the troops assembling for the Persian campaign, and gouging by Antiochene speculators. When Julian tried to set maximum prices for food and imported grain to relieve the shortage, the price fixing could not be enforced. Speculators bought up the grain and withheld it from the market, and merchants closed their shops to protest the price freeze.

Worse than that, no one supported the revival of paganism. When Julian went to Daphne for the great festival of Apollo, the local councillors stayed away, and even the people of Antioch were conspicuously absent. The emperor found at Daphne only the priest of Apollo equipped for sacrifice with a goose he had brought from home. The trouble was, Julian was told, that the Christian martyr Babylas was buried in the sacred grove so that the oracle of Apollo had been silenced and the whole precinct polluted. When the bones of Babylas were removed by imperial order and the sacred area purified, the temple of Apollo was shortly afterward consumed by flames: by a thunderbolt, some people said; by the Christians, others suspected. In the end, like some emperors before him, Julian decided that Antioch must be punished. Among other measures, he planned to move his headquarters to Tarsus so that the Antiochene profiteers could no longer fatten on the legions of Rome.

Libanius was in the middle of this, and he was no help to Julian. As a pagan, as a great orator, as a leading citizen of Antioch, Julian had counted on Libanius for support, but he knew little about Libanius. The two had not been teacher and pupil as some have believed. Julian knew Libanius by reputation only. He could not understand why Libanius did not rush to greet him when he arrived at the city gates as other important persons did. Libanius was playing his cards close to his chest: he says that he did not fawn on Julian because some property belonging to his grandfather had been confiscated and he did not wish to seem to be attempting to get it back; further, Libanius himself had fallen out of favor under Constantius, and again he did not want to come hat in hand for something that should be his without asking. So the orator was conspicuous by his absence. Julian invited him to lunch; Libanius replied that he didn't eat lunch, only dinner. When they finally got together, Libanius refused an offer of a government position and would discuss only academic matters with the emperor. When a showdown came between the councillors of Antioch and Julian, Libanius defended his fellow townspeople. Libanius was a supreme egotist, like most of his kind, or he was one of the great poker players of history—either way, he won.

As the fencing match finally ended, Libanius obliged the emperor with an oration:

> I was the last to take part, for the emperor himself had so devised it that there should be the fullest possible audience—that no single expression of mine should pass without its share of admiration. The Emperor contributed to this first by the pleasure which he expressed at my style, then by his tendency to rise to his feet in applause, until finally when he could no longer restrain himself, despite his best efforts, he leapt from his seat and with outstretched arms spread wide his cloak. Some of our boors would assert that in his excitement he forgot the dignity of his position, but anyone who is aware of what it is that makes kingship an object of reverence, would maintain that he stayed withing the bounds of what is proper. For what is more royal than that an emperor should be uplifted to the glory of eloquence.[7]

After more than six months Julian left Antioch to fight the Persians instead of his own subjects. In the beginning he was more successful, too, but after victories in major battles, he suffered a mortal wound in a minor skirmish.

So died Julian on the night of June 26, 363. The story that he lived until dawn and expired at sunrise exclaiming, "Pale Galilaean, thou hast conquered," is a late invention.

St. Gregory, his old schoolmate, rejoiced:

"The concluding reflection is for once appropriate—the liver of the victim was the appointed means of reading the future, and it was precisely in that organ that the arch-diviner received the final thrust."[8]

The Christian poet Prudentius was more charitable:

> Most brave leader and fashioner of laws
> Celebrated in speech and action
> Thoughtful of his country but not of religion
> Loving 300,000 gods but faithless to God
> Though faithful to the state.[9]

Eutropius, a pagan, said:

He was a remarkable man, and one that would have governed the empire with honor, if he had been permitted by the fates. He was eminently accomplished in liberal branches of knowledge, but better read in the literature of the Greeks, so much so that his Latin was by no means comparable to his Greek learning. He was possessed of a great and ready eloquence and a most tenacious memory. In some respects he was more like a philosopher than a prince. Towards his friends he was liberal, yet less discriminating as to the objects of his generosity than became so great an emperor; for there were some of them that cast a stain on his glory. To the people of the provinces he was most just, and remitted taxes on them as far as possible. He was indulgent towards all men; he felt no great anxiety about the public treasury, but of glory he was a great lover, and manifested even an intemperate desire for the attainment of it. He was a persecutor of the Christian religion yet so that he abstained from shedding blood. He was not unlike Marcus Aurelius whom he even studied to rival.[10]

Libanius honored the memory of Julian with a lament and an oration, both undistinguished, and an epitaph of two lines, one of which was lifted from Homer:

> Julian lies there beside the swift-flowing Tigris,
> Both a noble king and a brave warrior.

CHAPTER V

The Churchman

There was an ancient proverb, known even to the Sumerians, which said, "The life of today, it is the life of yesterday." Or, stated in more familiar form, "There is nothing new under the sun."

Sixteen centuries ago in 374 A.D. a churchman wrote, "A woman who deliberately destroys a foetus is answerable for murder. And any fine distinction as to its being completely formed or unformed is not admissible among us."

The Churchman was Basil the Great, founder of monastic discipline, and one of the people now to be encountered as our search for humanity brings us to three men—the Cappadocian Trinity—Basil, his brother Gregory of Nyssa, and their friend Gregory Nazianzus. Since the facts of their intertwined public lives are presumably well known, it will not be necessary to review on a large scale the biographies of each or to discuss their firmly Orthodox theology. For the Cappadocian Trinity we possess an unusual amount of information. Their combined orations, tracts, poems, and letters total many more than one thousand and take up ten volumes in Migne's *Patrology*, even in quarto with two columns to the page; letters alone number between seven and eight hundred items. Yet, what is so precious about this wealth of detail is the abundance of intimate, personal evidence that will permit us to penetrate the facade of greatness and to see these people as people. All three were canonized, and they earned it; for in spite of their ultimate triumph, they had more than their share of human frailty. In those days it was very hard to be a saint.

Whether Basil did indeed almost singlehanded stem the rising tide of Arianism under Valens and win the victory for Orthodoxy that came with Theodosius is difficult to say. Certainly he fought the good fight and won in Cappadocia. We can be more positive about his importance as the founder of what we know in the middle ages as monasticism: no one doubts that Greek, Russian, and Western monasticism were all indebted to him for their origin.

Like pilgrimage, fourth-century monasticism left something to be desired. Before Basil the ascetics, whether eremitic or cenobitic, had earned for themselves a reputation that was not universally favorable. According to one modern judgment:

"There is, perhaps, no phase in the moral history of mankind of a deeper and more painful interest than this ascetic epidemic. A hideous, sordid, emaciated maniac, without knowledge, without patriotism, without natural affection, passing his life in a long routine of useless and atrocious self torture, and quailing before the ghastly phantoms of his delirious brain had become the ideal of the nations which had known the writings of Plato and Cicero and the lives of Socrates and Cato."[1] The Gloomy Dean—they are all gloomy nowadays but you know the one I mean—called early monasticism "the strangest aberration in the history of the church."[2]

These are extreme views, based on a limited number of horrible examples, but we do hear contemporary fourth-century complaints of bands of monks roaming the countryside, pillaging the fields of helpless farmers. Eunapius, a pagan and hardly unbiased, called monks "men in appearance who led the lives of swine. In those days every man who wore a black robe and consented to behave in unseemly fashion in public possessed the power of a tyrant." In 379 in Constantinople, St. Gregory

Nazianzus was stoned by monks who broke into his church as he was celebrating the mass. Basil himself admits that all that glitters is not gold. In his youth he got in with the wrong crowd:

> I believed I had found an aid to my own salvation, and I considered the things that were seen as indications of things that were invisible. Since, therefore, the secret thoughts of each of us are unknown, I thought that lowliness of dress was sufficient evidence of lowliness of mind; and sufficient for my full assurance was the thick cloak and the girdle and the sandals of untanned hide.[3]

The ideal monk was a holy man who had renounced the world, disposed of his worldly goods, and subjected himself to severe self-discipline in his quest for the divine. He was the new philosopher belonging to a new self-proclaimed elite. In the monastic communities—or communes, if you like—there was hard physical labor at a primitive level and much talk of love—not of the erotic sort, of course. Monks were those in revolt against the establishment. Because they were only human there were some good and holy men, and others who merely talked a good game and were unprincipled charlatans. It is interesting that when organization and discipline did come and make something of monasticism, the pattern, *mirabile dictu*, was military, and the community was directed by an autocrat. As has been said, we should avoid garbing either the pilgrim or the monk of this early period in medieval attire.

To come to the Cappadocian Trinity, Basil was born in Caesarea Mazaca in 329. The family was well-to-do and staunchly Christian. Basil's father was a teacher of rhetoric and an advocate; his mother Emmelie was a person of great determination and strength only exceeded in these qualities by her eldest daughter, Macrina, ultimately St. Macrina, who was the mainstay of the family in later years and the founder of a nunnery which her mother also joined. Macrina, a great beauty, was engaged to be married at twelve, but the groom-to-be died, and she insisted on remaining a spinster. Besides Basil and Macrina, there were eight other children—four girls and four boys—including Gregory of Nyssa and the youngest boy, Peter, born after his father's death and raised at the knee of Macrina. Another brother, Naucratius, a most promising lad, was the victim of a "hunting" accident. He, like Basil, Macrina, Gregory, and Peter, might also have been canonized had he lived a bit longer.

Basil spent most of his childhood on the family estates in nearby Pontus, received his first advanced schooling in Caesarea, then went to Constantinople where he may have heard Libanius, and finally to Athens. He returned to Caesarea in 356 to teach rhetoric but after two years retired to Pontus to found a monastery and devise his famous rules for the monastic life. Incidentally, he was not baptized until 357 or 358 when he was nearly thirty years old.

The experiment with monasticism lasted only a few years, and then Basil returned to Caesarea to become an assistant to Bishop Eusebius. Efficient, aggressive, more than a bit pushy, he did not endear himself to old Eusebius and was dismissed. Very soon, however, as the Arians came into power under Valens, Basil was recalled and virtually ran the episcopal office until Eusebius died in 370. Although Basil succeeded the old man, his own tenure was difficult and stormy owing to Arian pressures and Basil's own ambition and conniving which we shall discuss later. He died in 379 just as Orthodoxy triumphed under Theodosius after the disaster or crowning mercy—whichever you prefer—of Adrianople.

Gregory of Nyssa, Basil's brother, was born in 331 or 335 and died in 395. Unlike the other two, Basil and Gregory Nazianzus, he did not study abroad but was educated at home, first by Macrina and then with advanced training at Caesarea, some of it from his brother Basil. Gregory was in and out of the church. Accepting a readership to please his mother, he resigned to teach rhetoric, then lived in a monastery for a while, then was appointed Bishop of Nyssa by Basil in 371 in a sort of court-packing deal to which we shall presently come. Unworldly, incredibly naïve, but sweet and well-intentioned, Gregory often made mistakes that caused him serious trouble. Deposed by the Arians and accused by the bureaucracy of misappropriating church funds, he spent some time in exile, but was later returned to his see, and, after the death of Basil and Gregory Nazianzus, he came into his own as a leading Orthodox theologian. Honored by the family of Theodosius, he was selected to pronounce the funeral orations of many of its members. His biography of his sister Macrina is one of the high spots of fourth-century literature.

Gregory of Nazianzus, born about the same time as Basil (329/330), died about 390. His birthplace was Arianzus near Diocaesarea, later called Nazianzus. He had a brother, Caesarius, a famous physician honored by Julian the Apostate even though Caesarius proudly proclaimed himself a Christian in the midst of the pagan reaction. There was a sister, Gorgonia, who in spite of her name was apparently not hideous since she did get married. Gregory's father, also named Gregory, began life as a member of the sect of the Hypsisterians, monotheists who rejected the trinity, sacrifices, any kind of ecclesiastical organization, observed the Jewish Sabbath and food taboos, and were definitely not Christians. But Nonna, Gregory's mother, converted her husband to Christianity—"grafted a wild olive tree onto a good one" as Gregory says—and père Gregory became Bishop of Nyssa. The young Gregory was educated at Caesarea, in Palestine, then Alexandria, and finally Athens where he spent ten years. He had known Basil slightly in Caesarea, but when Basil came to Athens, the two became fast friends. They maintained that they did not lead the rowdy lives of typical students but knew only two roads: one to class, and the other to church. Neither was baptized, however, until he returned home, and from the outset neither had any great commitment to the church.

Gregory says that on the way from Alexandria to Athens he nearly perished at sea, was rescued by Phoenician sailors and vowed something or other to the deity, yet it was a long time before he got around to fulfill it. On his return home from Athens he tried the monastic life with Basil but did not find it to his liking. He went home, could not make up his mind what he wanted to do, was dragooned into the priesthood by his father at a moment when he was off-guard, and then, like Gregory of Nyssa, used by Basil in his politicking as bishop. We shall come to a fuller explanation of this, but for now it is enough to say that Gregory of Nazianzus, like Gregory of Nyssa, carried on after Basil's death. This Gregory was the most likable of the three. He had a sense of humor, sometimes too much for his own good. He hated committees (i.e., synods), and all he wanted was to be left alone to work things out for himself. He was a bishop; he had a church in Constantinople; he filled in at Nazianzus after that; and then retired. He was not an organization man.

❖❖❖❖❖❖❖❖❖❖❖❖❖

The beginning is the story of Basil and Gregory, classmates at Athens, where their close friendship actually started. It was there that they came to know a fellow student named Julian. Gregory was able to endure most people, even if he did not like them, but not Julian. Whatever it was that Julian did, he made a lifelong enemy of Gregory. We cannot accept Gregory's later story that already in Athens he divined the menace of Julian, that he said, "What an evil the Roman state is nourishing." Julian's imperial prospects were then something less than zero; because of the high mortality of his relatives, he would have been a poor risk for life insurance.

In Athens Basil and Gregory made great plans for the future, the things they would do together when they went home, but their dreams were never realized. Basil came back to Caesarea, says Gregory of Nyssa, "where he had had practice in rhetoric for a long time. He was excessively puffed up by his rhetorical abilities and disdainful of all great reputations, and considered himself better than the leading men of the district."[7] After sister Macrina took him down a few notches, Basil decided to retire from the world to his own monastery although first he made a trip to Palestine and Egypt to see how it was done.

He then set up camp on family property in Pontus on the banks of the Iris River just across the stream from his mother and sister. In a glowing letter to his friend Gregory Nazianzus Basil described the beauties of the site: a plain protected by rushing waters on two sides and a mountain on another; there were flowers and birds; fish in the river; and it was quiet with no visitors except for a chance hunter.

Gregory joined Basil briefly. One gathers from his recollections of their experience that is was not unlike that of the nineteenth-century utopians or of many young people of today who set out to tame the wilderness in order to make a better world. There was a lot of blood, sweat, frustration, and inconvenience.

Gregory found that the Iris River site did not live up to Basil's prospectus. It was clothed in a chronic fog and chill so that Basil's followers might well be called the Cimmerians of Pontus. There were thorn thickets everywhere to lacerate the flesh; the river was full of stones, not fish, and the noise of its torrent made psalm-singing or conversation inaudible. The birds did sing, it was true, but from hunger rather than joy; and the hunters came, not to hunt animals, but to search for the corpses of the monks. Gregory also added:

> Your roofless and doorless hut, your fireless and smokeless hearth, your walls dried by fire, that we may not be hit by the drops of the mud —we young and miserable survivors of a wreck. For I remember those loaves and the broth . . . and my poor teeth that slipped on your hunks of bread, and then braced themselves up, and pulled themselves as it were out of the mud . . . for if we had not been quickly delivered by that great supporter of the poor—I mean your mother—who appeared opportunely like a harbor to men tossed by a storm, we should long ago have been dead, rather pitied than admired for our faith in Pontus. How shall I pass over that garden which was no garden and had no vegetables.[5]

Basil came back to the world to assist Bishop Eusebius, as we have seen, but then was dismissed. Gregory tried hard to reconcile the two, writing first to Basil stressing the difficulty of the times and the need for working together, offering to go to Bishop Eusebius to heal the breach. He also wrote several letters to Eusebius, but the old man was adamant and even attacked Gregory for what he felt was meddling and behaving in an insolent manner.

Eusebius did recall Basil, and when the aged prelate died, Basil became Bishop of Caesarea, but not without a little political maneuvering. The election was not a foregone conclusion, so Basil, needing the votes of both Gregories, father and son, and knowing that the younger Gregory would not willingly play his game, feigned illness. When he hurried to Caesarea and then discovered he had been tricked, Gregory was bitter:

> What your object was I cannot guess, or how my presence was going to achieve it. . . . There is nothing I prize higher than your life, and no blow that could be so severe as your death. . . . I had every detail of your funeral arranged. However, when I noticed the bishops gathering into the city, my haste received a check. I began to wonder. I wondered first of all at your insufficient realization of what was fitting in this matter and at your failure to guard against popular gossip, which is so swift to denigrate the purest of intentions. In the second place it surprised me that you should consider a similar line of conduct suitable for both of us, to whom life, learning, everything is in common, in that God set his seal on our association from the beginning. Thirdly I was surprised that you should consider such elections the business of pious men, and not, as they are, the business of power-mongers, who are concerned with popular favor.[6]

When Valens came to power and began to promote the Arian cause, one of his stratagems was to split Cappadocia (Basil's see) into two dioceses. Basil was left in charge of one, but the other was packed with Arian appointees. To counter this move Basil created new bishops of his own. These included his brother Gregory who was sent to Nyssa and his friend Gregory Nazianzus who was assigned to Sasima, a small and thoroughly unattractive hamlet in the middle of nowhere. Friend Gregory refused to play the game and was utterly uncooperative so that a quarrel broke out between him and Basil in which harsh words were exchanged. Gregory resented being used for what he considered purely political purposes, and he was offended by Basil's high and mighty episcopal tone which he thought hardly suitable for correspondence between friends. He said, "I have been put upon . . . and I blame this matter of a bishopric, which has suddenly given you airs. I am tired of having to answer for your mistakes, of defending you to people who are under no illusion about the change in our relationship. . . . I am at the same time wronged and put in the wrong."[7]

Nevertheless, Gregory remained fiercely loyal to Basil when the latter was attacked by gossip-mongers. In a letter to Basil, he wrote:

There is a party here at which a great many distinguished friends of ours were present, and amongst them was a man who wore the name and dress which betoken piety (a monk). They had not yet begun to drink, but were talking about us, as often happens at such parties, and made us rather than anything else the subject of their conversation. They admired everything connected with you, and they brought me in as professing the same philosophy; and they spoke of our friendship . . . and of our conformity of views and feelings on all points. Our philosopher was annoyed by this. "What is this, gentlemen?" he said, with a mighty shout, "what liars and flatterers you are. You may praise these men for other reasons if you like, and I will not contradict you; but I cannot concede to you the most important point, their orthodoxy. Basil and Gregory are falsely praised; the former, because his words are a betrayal of the faith, the latter, because his toleration aids the treason.[8]

Gregory stoutly defended his friend, but he felt compelled to report the incident to Basil, saying, "What I write now I write unwillingly, but still I write it. . . . Please forgive me for writing it out of goodwill to you."

In the meantime Basil was learning about another side of episcopal administration. From his letters we know that he was plagued by mundane problems that were neither theological nor political. His assistants, the chorepiscopi, were discovered taking money from candidates for ordination. A priest kept a woman in his household and had to be commanded to put her in a convent and get a manservant instead. Basil had to write to the governor of Cappadocia asking for the arrest of a creditor who had broken into his house, caused the death of a servant, beaten women servants, and carried off whatever he pleased. Clergy who came for a synod stole from one another. And so on.

Nevertheless, there is a lighter side in some of the letters ascribed to Basil. As for example, the one addressed to a calligrapher:

Write straight and keep straightly to your lines; and let the hand neither mount upwards nor slide downhill. Do not force the pen to travel slantwise . . . but proceed straight ahead as if traveling along a carpenter's rule . . . For that which is slantwise is unbecoming, but that which is straight is a joy to those who see it, not permitting the eyes of those who read to bob up and down like well-sweeps.[9]

Or the exchange of letters with the governor Antipater:

Basil: "I hear you have revived your failing appetite with sauerkraut."
Antipater: "Cabbage is twice death, says the proverb, but as for me though I have often asked for death, I shall die but once even though I did not ask for it, but sauerkraut is not so bad."[10]

Gregory Nazianzus, on the other hand, was generally more relaxed and playful—if we can accept some of the letters as genuine. In a letter to Amphilochus, a friend of the whole Cappadocian Trinity:

I did not ask for bread any more than I would look for water from the people of Ostracine. But it is not extraordinary nor contrary to friendship to ask you, a man of Ozizala, for vegetables of which you have an enormous abundance. . . . So make up your mind to send me some and plenty of them and of the best quality for I am about to receive the great Basil, and you who know him when he is full and philosophical would not like to see him hungry and cross.[11]

Or to Theodore of Tyana:

You summon me! I come at once, but strictly for a private visit to you alone. Synods and conventions I salute from afar for I know from experience that most of them are sorry affairs, to say the least.[12]

In addition to the letters, the epigrams of Gregory Nanzianzus were famous and treasured. The surviving epigrams number more than two hundred and fifty. They are mostly sepulchral, but the variety of their subjects is interesting and revealing as will be seen later. Almost one hundred have to do with tomb robbers, violators of tombs, and those who feast in the churches of the martyrs. More than fifty are devoted to his mother, father, and members of his family and the family of Basil. There is a curious one about Gorgonia who had malaria and prayed herself out of it, and one explains the "hunting accident" of Naucratius, the brother of Basil and Gregory of Nyssa:

"Naucratius caught in the fetters of his net was released from the fetters of this life while fishing."[13]

Through the letters of all three Cappadocians run common themes. One has to do with the bad weather—cold in winter, and frequently damp in summer. Another plays on the subject of illness: all three think they are chronically at death's door and frequently use ill-health as an excuse for not doing something or making a long trip. Astrology and fortune-telling are frequently mentioned, as they are by other fourth-century persons, and one finds in addition the same kind of love for the countryside that pervades the letters of Julian or the orations of Libanius.

As for Gregory of Nyssa specifically, a number of his letters describe in fulsome detail the landscape and extraordinary buildings, villas and chapels, erected by his wealthy friends. In a letter to Amphilochus he goes on at some length about an octagonal structure resembling the Golden House of Constantine at Antioch:

The form of the chapel is a cross, which has its figure completed throughout, as you would expect by four structures. The junctions of the buildings intercept one another, as we see everywhere in the cruciform pattern. But within the cross there lies a circle, divided by eight angles (I call the octagonal figure a circle in view of its circumference) in such wise that the two pairs of sides of he octagon which are diametrically opposed to one another unite by means of arches the central circle to the adjoining blocks of building; while the other four sides of the octagon, which lie between the quadrilateral buildings, will not themselves be carried to meet the buildings, but upon each of them will be described in a semicircle like a shell, terminating in an arch above.[14]

Most famous, of course, is the long letter to the family friend Olympius in which he tells of the death and funeral of his sister Macrina. Gregory had gone to Jerusalem to fulfill a vow and "to see the evidence of our Lord's sojourn in the flesh," but the trip was disappointing, and on his way back he made a detour to visit Macrina. She was dying. They had a little time to talk about the family and their own doings, and then she expired. Gregory describes the funeral, attended by all the people of the area, great and small. She was interred in the family tomb, and Gregory in a macabre passage tells of his unhappy experience in having to open the tomb and view the bodies of his father and mother.

To sum up:

They were human. Basil the organizer, the driver, ambitious and impatient; Gregory, his friend, who wanted no fame, no responsibility; the other Gregory, Basil's brother, a good and gentle soul, who was the real philosopher of the three, though he had never been to Athens.

Like Julian, they were the victims of a divided culture, torn by their classical education and its goals and their devotion to Christianity and its demands. Julian had tried to reconcile it all by creating a pagan church on the Christian model, and Basil in his famous treatise on the education of young men sought a compromise between the classical and what he felt was a proper Christian education, a subject treated by Werner Jaeger in his epilogue to the *Paideia*.[15]

Basil and Gregory Nazianzus had difficulty deciding whether to be monks or priests. Basil chose the life of action, and Gregory yearned more and more for the seclusion of the cloister. At first he hoped he had made the proper choice when he yielded to his father's wishes and resolved to devote himself

to saving the world, but it didn't work for him. He got none of
the satisfaction that Basil derived from directing and manipu-
lating other people. Gregory's final address to the Council at
Constantinople in 381 is poignant. He had been one of the candidates for the vacant patriarchate, but tired of the wrangling
of the bishops he resigned, saying:

> My lords, God has brought you together so that you may determine
> something that He would wish. As for my own affairs, let them take
> second place; for, in the business of such an important assembly, it is
> really trivial what the outcome be (of his own affairs), even though my
> elevation has been in vain. You should elevate your minds to a higher
> consideration. You are actually met together; then, even though it be
> the eleventh hour, decide eventually to be together. How long can we
> go on being a laughing stock? People regard us as insensitive creatures
> devoid of any feelings except combat. Please join hands with a good will
> in a gesture of fellowship. I am become Jonas the prophet. I am giving
> myself as victim for the safety of the ship, even though it will be a case
> of the innocent encountering the waves. Take me then, on the issue of
> the lot, and cast me forth. The hospitable whale will welcome me in the
> depths. From now on begin to be of one mind, and then make your way
> towards everything in due order. Let this place be known as the place of
> openness, and I will then have played not an ignoble part. If you persist
> with me, I shall have a single criticism — that you are making a contest
> over thrones. If you take the view that I suggest, nothing will be difficult.
> When I was enthroned it was without enthusiasm, and now I take my
> leave with a will. My state of health suggests this course too. I have only
> one death to die and this is in the hands of God. But, O My Trinity, you
> are all I care for! What tongue will you have, trained for your defence?
> An independent one I hope and full of zeal! Fare you well, my lords,
> and be mindful of my labours.[16]

CHAPTER VI

The Soldier
and the Grammarian

These chapters may have seemed to you formless and without plan, but I should like to remind you that geographically we have traveled from one end of the empire to the other with the Pilgrim of 333, gone beyond the Euphrates to visit Shapur, toured Antioch with Julian, and penetrated Cappadocia with Basil and the two Gregories. Now we come to Egypt.

In addition, I might mention that we have, as promised, used sources of varied kinds: inscriptions, law codes, ancient monuments, archaeological materials, formal histories, treatises, orations, and letters. On this occasion we shall get our data from poetry and papyri.

Finally, we have made the acquaintance of many different people: a Roman emperor, a barbarian king, prominent churchmen, an anonymous pilgrim, an orator, and numerous other persons including women as well as men, pagans as well as Christians. Moving on, the names of those we are about to meet are not to be found in the pages of formal histories or in the annals of the church, certainly not the unhappy teacher of grammar who was a poet in spite of himself nor the professional soldier who spent most of his forty years in the army as an enlisted man but finally rose to the exalted rank of lieutenant or captain.

As for the land of Egypt, one might say that like Gaul it could be divided into three parts: the Delta or Lower Egypt, the Valley or Upper Egypt, and the Fayum, an oasislike region just west of the Nile at about the junction of Upper and Lower Egypt. Although this tripartite division is basically a topographic one, it could also be maintained that in the Greco-Roman period there were, culturally speaking, two Egypts: one, the city of Alexandria, the political, intellectual, and religious capital of the country; the other, the *chora* or country that comprised the rest of Egypt and where life was quite different from that of urban Alexandria. We shall visit both city and country.

Alexandria, founded by Alexander the Great, had become a center of learning and culture famous for its scholars, its school of medicine, and its large Jewish community where once the great Philo lived. Alexandria was a huge city, larger than Antioch, rivaling Rome in size, and it had the usual urban problem: a riotous population. Long before the Romans the Greco-Macedonian Ptolemies, forebears of Cleopatra who ruled Egypt, had been forced to exploit the palliative effects of bread and circuses. In the fourth century A.D., almost seven hundred years after the founding of their city, the Alexandrines were still unrully. They fought among themselves, not over chariot races and other ephemera as of yore, but over questions of theology. In the days of Constantine the partisans of Athanasius and Arius brawled in the streets; in the time of Julian the city mob butchered George the book-lover, a fitting end for one who had begun his career in an abatoir; later, a frenzied crowd martryed Hypatia, the pagan nun, the bride of science.

A fair sample of goings-on in Alexandria is provided by a papyrus letter written in 335 A.D. It describes an affair involving Athanasius but not Arius. Instead, it has to do with the contest between the Orthodox faction and the schismatics of Meletius. The original dispute which had begun about thirty years before between Bishop Peter and Bishop Meletius was not over a matter of theology but of policy. How should the *lapsi*, those Christians who had defected during the great persecution

instituted by Diocletian, be treated? Should they be readmitted
to the church with only slight penance or should they be subjected to more severe discipline? Peter and Meletius, the primor-
dial antagonists, were dead by 335, and the fundamental cause
of the dissension was pretty well forgotten; but now there was
an Orthodox church with its bishops and a Meletian church,
the church of the martyrs, with its own hierarchy. The surviving
Meletians were mostly Copts, native Egyptians, naturally hostile to the Greco-Roman elite of Alexandria. In 335 Athanasius
was under attack by the increasingly powerful Arians at court
in Constantinople, yet he found time to carry on the feud with
the Meletians inherited from his predecessor. The Meletian
side of the incident of 335 is given in the papyrus letter:[1]

One of the Meletian bishops came to Alexandria and entered
the *praetorium* to dine there with a fellow bishop. The Atha-
nasian faction came hunting for him after enlisting the aid of a
few drunken soldiers. Some soldiers, favorably disposed toward
the Meletians, hid the bishop and his attendants in store cham-
bers, while the Athanasians, wild with rage at losing their quarry,
found other Meletian brethren, beat them, "and made them
all bloody." Still others were arrested in a hostel nearby and
taken to the camp, but the next morning they were released
with apologies by the pagan Roman officer responsible for
their detention; he had sobered up and apparently realized
that it was not his business to take sides in Egyptian disputes
and especially not to favor the partisans of Athanasius whose
future was so uncertain.

The letter goes on to list the names of Meletian bishops and
priests either under arrest or expelled from the country by
Athanasius; Athanasius himself was said to be prepared to flee
from Egypt should news of an Arian victory come from Constantinople.

As the Christians fought among themselves, the pagans in
Alexandria clung to their old ways but recognized that their
cause was lost. Typical of this other aspect of life in the great
city are the views expressed by the poet Palladas in his epigrams

which are now to be found scattered through the Greek Anthology, and it is from these verses that we can also learn the facts of his own essentially gloomy existence.

The Greek Anthology, it will be recalled, is a great collection of Greek epigrams—convivial, satirical, sepulchral, amatory, and declamatory—a combination of three earlier compilations dating from the first century B.C. and the second and sixth centuries A.D. respectively. Barring a few epigrams of Julian and Libanius and the separate collection of epigrams of Gregory Nazianzus, the poems of Palladas reveal him as the only major figure of the anthology dating from the fourth century. He has, in fact, been called the most considerable Greek poet of the period between the reign of Marcus Aurelius and that of Justinian. One hundred and seventy-five of his epigrams remain, and in his lifetime he was well known, even honored by having one of his poems recorded by a graffito in a latrine at Ephesus.

Palladas seems to have been born in Egypt about 350. This would make him a contemporary of the poet Claudian, also Egyptian-born, but there the parallel ends. Claudian left Egypt for Rome where he wrote Latin poetry, became the poet laureate of the court of Honorius, gained senatorial rank, and married a rich wife. Palladas, on the other hand, stayed behind in Egypt barely ekeing out a living as a teacher of grammar, poverty striken, and married to an equally impoverished shrew. These matters and others come out of the epigrams.

Palladas as a grammaticus, an elementary teacher, was neither happy nor successful. Somehow he had to instruct unwilling youngsters in Greek grammar and induce them to understand, even to love, Greek poetry. One began, of course, with Homer, with the first five lines of the *Iliad*:

> Goddess, sing the wrath of Achilles Peleades,
> Baneful, that laid upon the Achaeans ten thousand woes
> And sent to Hades the many strong souls of heroes
> With carcasses left behind as spoil for dogs
> And birds. Thus the will of Zeus was fulfilled . . .

As Palladas put it:

> The beginning of grammar is a curse in five lines.
> The first has wrath; the second baneful
> And then many woes; the third leads down many souls to Hades;
> The fourth has spoil for dogs; and the fifth
> Birds of ill omen and the anger of Zeus.
> How then can a grammarian avoid
> Having many sorrows after 5 curses and 5 cases?[2]

Not only did Palladas detest his occupation, but also it was far from remunerative. He complained that parents would promise to pay a certain amount for a year's instruction at the end of the term, and then they would trick him by withdrawing their child after eleven months to avoid paying anything at all. In other cases, servants entrusted with the money to pay the tuition in installments would exchange good money for inferior currency while on the way to the school and pocket the difference.

All in all, it left much to be desired, and to cap the climax Palladas lost his job. Even before that mishap, he had just been scraping along financially:

> Parsing has brought me to a pretty pass.
> I'll sell my books and turn my muse to grass,
> For if I don't, I plainly see
> That presently she'll be the death of me.[3]

And out of work, he wrote:

> I'll sell my Pindar. Who will buy
> And with him all the rules of cases?
> For mine's a case of poverty
> That won't admit a poet's graces.
> I'd better go to some kind friend
> And ask him for commiseration.
> Perhaps a buck or two he'll lend,
> Or else "to starve" will be my conjugation.[4]

It was bad enough to be unemployed, but it was even worse to try to cope with the situation at home.

I can't afford a wife and grammar, too.
Grammar that is unrewarding and a wife unjust!
What I suffer from both is Death and Fate.
I have just escaped from grammar,
But I can't get away from this Andromache (man-fighter)
For our marriage contract and Roman law forbid it.[5]

But he got his revenge in one of his best and most famous epigrams:

Every woman is a source of annoyance,
But she has two good seasons:
One *en thalamo* (in the marriage chamber); the other
en thanato (in the grave).[6]

The verses of Palladas dwell on others of his favorite themes as well. Poverty, the bureaucracy, the Christians in general, and monks in particular roused his ire. Money, he said, was the child of pain and care: "It's fear to have you and pain not to." One of his epigrams is reminiscent of an old Sumerian proverb about the poor man who has meat but no salt, and when he has salt he has no meat, etc.:

A poor man has never lived
And he does not even die,
For when he seemed alive,
He was really like a corpse.[7]

On the bureaucracy:

No magistrate ever came here who was both clean-handed
and mild.
For one principle is hostile to the other.
Mildness is a virtue of the thief and purity a virtue
of the proud.
These are the two instruments of the government.[8]

Another epigram pillories the prefect who wept crocodile tears as he stole from his subjects, and several deal with a minor official named Gessius who died of disappointment after failing to achieve the high office that the astrologers had predicted for him.

On the Christians:

> All the world is upside down.
> Hope is buried, none to save.
> Ghosts we Greeks who walk the town,
> Ashes on our grave.[9]

In another, the discredited Heracles comes to Palladas in a dream and tells him sagely that "even a god must learn to serve the times."

In his epigram on monks Palladas plays on the word *monachos* (solitary):

> If solitaries, why so many?
> If so many, how are they solitaries?
> O crowd of solitaries
> Who make a mockery of solitude![10]

Among the satirical epigrams Palladas cannot resist the traditional targets: doctors, actors, and dancers. It was better, he said, to be judged by Hegemon, the slayer of robbers, than to fall prey to the surgeon, Gennadius. Hegemon executed murderers justly, but Gennadius took a fee for sending his patients down to Hades. Memphis, the monkey-nose, danced the parts of Daphne and Niobe; his Daphne was wooden and his Niobe like stone. Menander appeared to the comedian Paulus in a dream and said, "I never did you any harm, but you speak me ill." The cleverest of all is one in which Palladas makes fun of his profession:

> A grammarian's daughter having known a man
> Produced a child which was masculine, feminine, and
>   neuter.[11]

Like Marcus Aurelius—and many others, of course—Palladas was oppressed by the fear of death. Bravely whistling in the dark on one occasion he proclaimed that there was no suffering beyond the grave, but in another epigram he says, "We are all kept and fed for death like a herd of swine to be butchered without reason."

How much of the real Palladas the epigrams reveal to us is difficult to determine. Many of his attitudes are typical of his age, and perhaps his most biting satires are the product of his craft rather than an expression of his personality. One recalls his pleasure at the successful grafting of a pear tree in his garden and his playful dig at Olympius, who had promised him a horse but instead brought "a tail with an expiring nag dangling at the other end." And a far cry from the satirical is his tender sepulchral epigram referring to what must have been a shocking tragedy:

> He carried off a bride, and Fate carried off the
>   wedding party,
>   despoiling of life the happy company.
> One wedding sent four and twenty corpses to
>   the grave,
>   and one chamber was their common tomb.
> Penthesilea, unhappy bride, and Pentheus, bridegroom of
>   sorrow, rich in death was your marriage.[12]

For a much different scene and subject we shall now go from the city to the country, from Egypt proper into the Fayum, from poetry to prose, and most particularly to the papyri and the contents of an archive.

Despite difficulties of arrangement, gaps which almost always seem to involve key documents, and everybody's rotten handwriting, anyone who has worked on the papers of an individual, a family, or a business, military, political, or some other organization knows that it can be fun and ordinarily very satisfying. If the papers are old enough, one can maintain a pose of innocent virtue. What harm can there be in a little antiquarian gossip-mongering, in discovering the skeletons in someone's closet, especially if the remains are practically fossilized?

This is certainly the case with Abinnaeus the soldier. Wherever he began, Abinnaeus ended his career in the Fayum, the oasis fed by a branch of the Nile. Comprising about one-tenth of the arable land of Egypt, the Fayum possessed a sizable population in the Greco-Roman period with a hundred villages dotting its landscape. By the fourth century A.D. depopulation had set in, however, and the villages were gradually abandoned. It would be a millennium and a half before the Egyptians would return to reclaim this fertile region, but for modern scholarship this was hardly a disaster. Tens of thousands of Greek and Latin papyri were preserved virtually intact in the dry ruins of the villages, and European and American scholars were fortunate enough to arrive in Egypt in time to save many of these documents from destruction as the Fayum was being reoccupied in the nineteenth century.

The papyri deal with varied matters. There are all kinds of governmental and private documents as well as the valuable literary papyri which have given us long-lost texts of Sappho, Menander, Aristotle, and a host of other authors, some still unidentified. Many archives, both public and private, have been discovered and studied. Most famous, perhaps, is the Zenon archive of the third century B.C., but there are numerous others, and the Abinnaeus archive is one of the three important ones from the fourth century; the other two are those of Aurelius Isidorus and Sakaon, both large landholders.

The Abinnaeus archive comprises eighty-two papyri.[13] About half of these are from the official and private correspondence of Flavius Abinnaeus, a former cavalry officer, and the rest — petitions, contracts, accounts, legal documents — are relics of his tour of duty in the Fayum and the private papers of his wife, Nonna. There is no way to gauge the number of papyri in the original archive since it was found by native Egyptian farmers in 1892, not as the result of formal archaeological excavation. Only the best peices were conveyed to a dealer in Cairo who in turn hawked fifty-one to the British Museum and twenty-nine to the University Library of Geneva, Switzerland. Two other papyri were acquired probably from the same dealer: one by Pierre Jouguet as he was reassembling the Sakaon archive; and one by Bouriant, another French papyrologist. There are undoubtedly other scraps from the archive in various collections but unidentified as such.

At any rate, the whole story of the Abinnaeus archive is interesting and typical: a clandestine discovery, competing buyers falling all over one another, the dealer holding back some pieces to raise prices, and so on. One thing seems certain, and that is that the papyri were not found at Dionysias, the fort in the western Fayum where Abinnaeus was in command. Dionysias was excavated in 1898/9 by Grenfell and Hunt and again in 1948/50 by a Franco-Swiss expedition, but not a scrap of papyrus was found. Since the papers include documents belonging to Abinnaeus' wife relating to affairs at Philadelphia in the eastern Fayum where Abinnaeus retired, it seems most probable that Philadelphia rather than Dionysias was the find spot. Philadelphia, you may remember, was where the Zenon papyri were found and dispersed; bits and pieces of that archive are still turning up.

Dionysias had a huge fort, 240 x 210 yards in extent with walls twenty feet high. A street led from the only gate on the north to a big building, the quarters of the commandant and the soldiers of the garrison who were housed in some fifty rooms. There was no real necessity in that peaceful era for a fort of such size and strength, but it was a product of the standardization introduced by Diocletian; hundreds of forts just like it were built all over the empire. It was simpler to have a single plan, and Diocletian was great on uniformity.

At Dionysias Abinnaeus was the *praefectus castororum* (*eparch*) in command of the *ala* or unit of cavalry stationed there. The principal duties of the garrison were to act against brigands and smugglers and perform general police duties, provide escorts for imperial officials, assist in the collection of taxes, and carry on recruiting by press-gang tactics. Abinnaeus was also for the local people a kind of justice of the peace although serious cases were referred to his superior, the Dux in Alexandria, commander-in-chief of all Egyptian forces, who also held the rank of Count.

Flavius Abinnaeus was born about the beginning of Diocletian's reign (284/5) and joined the army at the end of that reign (305). After thirty years we find Abinnaeus in Egypt in command of a cavalry troop of non-Roman archers of eastern origin (Parthusagittarii) stationed in Upper Egypt near the southern frontier. He was called upon in 337/8 to escort an embassy of the barbarian tribe of the Blemmyes to Constantinople. As a reward for this service Abinnaeus was promoted to *protector* and ordered to conduct the embassy back to Africa. This turned out to be a three-year undertaking, and in recognition of his accomplishment of the mission and because he was nearing retirement Abinnaeus was given the post at Dionysias, a sinecure before his termination of service. When he presented his orders at Alexandria at the office of the Dux, however, he discovered that several other people had received similar orders to command at Dionysias. Abinnaeus then wrote in Latin an official letter to the emperors Constantius and Constans protesting that he had earned the duty at Dionysias and that his rivals had been appointed through patronage by high bureaucratic officials. He won his case and served at the fort for two years (342-44) when suddenly the new Dux, Valacius, discharged him. Valacius said (in Latin):

> . . . a successor to you has been appointed, since it is supposed that you have reached the term of your command. Your successor is . . . (name lost). Hand over to him instantly the soldiers of the *ala* . . . as well as the imperial ensigns and the intact inventory of the men's equipment. Take care also to instruct him in all the rules to be followed to guarantee public safety, in order to safeguard him from hesitation and mistakes, at any rate in the early days of his tenure. After you have taken these steps and laid down your command you may attend to your own interests.[14]

No quitter and well aware of his rights, Abinnaeus made a trip to Constantinople to lay his case before the emperor again. He was reinstated and served another hitch at Dionysias (346-51) when he finally retired at about age sixty-five.

The letter to Constantius and Constans and the letter from Valacius are in Latin, but the rest of the documents of the archive are in Greek. Most date from 346. Among other things they reveal great uncertainty about the right name of Abinnaeus and his ultimate origin. His name is spelled twelve different ways in the papyri, and in one form or another they support the hypothesis that he was an Italian, a Syrian, or even an Egyptian because in the latter case the form "Ammeneus" could be translated "Amon has come." We are on somewhat firmer ground when we come to Abinnaeus' family which the papyri tell us consisted of his wife Nonna and two sons, named Constantius and Domnus.

Of the forty-two letters in the archive, thirty-seven are addressed to Abinnaeus. They come from officials of various kinds, from soldiers of equal rank with Abinnaeus himself, from veterans, from friends and clients, and from business connections. There are twenty-six different correspondents in all. Some documents are written by the same scribe for several different people; some are from the same people using different scribes. Some of Abinnaeus' correspondents are Christians; others, most in fact, are pagans. It is uncertain whether Abinnaeus was a Christian; he gives no indication of it, and he was on equally friendly terms with both Christians and pagans. The epistolary forms are a little vague, but usually a superior writing to an inferior will say "From X to Y (the inferior)," and an inferior will say "To X from Y (the inferior)." Equals call Abinnaeus *adelphos* (brother); inferiors address him as patron, *despotes* (master), or *kyrios* (lord). It is interesting that when Abinnaeus went to Constantinople to protest his dismissal by Valacius he carried letters or petitions to the emperor from a number of people, mostly those wanting jobs for themselves or for relatives. This seems to bespeak considerable confidence in the ability of Abinnaeus to get things done.

A sampling of Abinnaeus' correspondence will suggest that he did not have the easiest job in the world. Flavius Macarius, "most illustrious Overseer of the Imperial Domains," writes him a blustering letter saying that the "most illustrious Count and Duke" has given orders that a detachment from Dionysias should be supplied to assist in the collection of the imperial taxes. If Abinnaeus fails to send soldiers, the matter will be brought to the attention of the Duke who will not be pleased that Abinnaeus has "impeded the collection of imperial revenues." One suspects that no such orders had been issued by the Duke and that Macarius was trying to make things easier for himself by intimidating the taxpayers with a military escort. Quite the opposite of this is found in a letter from an official named Demetrius, more or less equal in rank with Abinnaeus, who has requested aid in halting the smuggling of natron from the desert into Egypt. Natron was long an imperial monopoly and had to be purchased by the consumers from the government, but Egyptians as well as desert dwellers were smuggling the material in and must be apprehended and their natron confiscated. Demetrius has already written one letter to Abinnaeus which has gone unacknowledged; therefore, this new communication is carried by a special messenger. Demetrius assumes politely that Abinnaeus did not receive the first letter.

A priest named Mios, a Christian, writes frequently to Abinnaeus in the most cordial and familiar terms. He has numerous favors to request but never fails to accompany his letters with gifts. On one occasion Mios asks for nets to trap the gazelles who are destroying the crops. If Abinnaeus does not have any nets, perhaps he can find some, suggests Mios. He says further that he is sending Abinnaeus the skin of a hyena.

A fellow officer asks Abinnaeus to take action in the case of a soldier whose son has been attacked by native children armed with clubs and swords. A landholder, charged with the responsibility of collecting the grain tax complains that he has been attacked by a drunken soldier belonging to Abinnaeus' command; he makes his complaint to Abinnaeus first rather than going to the commanding officer in his own district. A veteran has been robbed and asks Abinnaeus to force the village officials to seek out and apprehend the culprits. Kaor, village priest of Hermopolis, begs Abinnaeus to forgive the desertion of the soldier Paul, but subsequently another villager from Hermopolis reports that Paul has sheared his sheep during the night and made off with six of his pigs. Another report of nocturnal sheep-shearing comes in from a different village a week later, but this time Paul is not involved in the crime. A deacon of the "principal church" in Berenicis complains that a villager from Philagris has stolen his clothes and shamelessly wears them in public.

As "master and patron" Abinnaeus receives petitions as well as police reports. A Christian named Thareotes prays for the health of Abinnaeus' sons, Constantius and Domnus, and then commends his nephew to the attention of Abinnaeus. In the hope that the favor will be granted Thareotes is sending jars of quails, fish paste, and grape syrup as well as some chickens.

And so it went.

It may be that the papyri tell us more about the job than the man; but, unlike the tortured, writhing Palladas, Abinnaeus seems secure, stable, and well-adjusted. He is a professional; he knows his job and his rights. He has chosen the military, accepts its rules and regulations, and after forty years is content. Dionysias, on the edge of the badlands, was not a great billet, but for a cavalry officer it was probably nice just to sit down and handle routine matters of administration that he knew so well. Abinnaeus was on top of most situations. Without any fuss and feathers he had performed a diplomatic mission escorting the barbarian chieftains to Constantinople and back. Later, he returned to Constantinople to face down the bureaucracy. He had the respect and friendship of fellow officers, and he had established good, even intimate, relations with the Fayum peasants, Christians and pagans alike. We can imagine a friendly going-away party when he finally relinquished his command. People were no doubt flattered that he did not leave the Fayum but bought a little house in Philadelphia for his retirement years. As for Abinnaeus, it was something he could afford and probably better than he had anticipated in his younger days. It all belonged to the pattern of his life and was therefore reassuring and comfortable.

CHAPTER VII

The Man of Affairs

One of the most human, believable, likeable people in our
Fourth Century was Synesius of Cyrene, a younger contemporary of Libanius and the Cappadocian Trinity. Not a prima
donna and poseur like Libanius, not striving to make his mark
like Ammianus Marcellinus, not warped by religion or partisan-
ship like so many others we have encountered, Synesius just
sailed along in his well-adjusted, even-tempered way, and yet
without the usual contortions, hornblowing, and publicity-
seeking he earned a few pages rather than a footnote in the
great book of history.

Synesius was thoroughly Greek and proud to be from "La-
conian" Cyrene, that region west of Egypt on the Mediterranean coast settled by colonists from the Peloponnesus in the
seventh century B.C. The chronological details of his busy life
are a bit hazy, but he seems to have been born about 370, and
he died in 413 or shortly thereafter. Versatile, or perhaps more
properly jack-of-all-trades, Synesius began life as a pagan and
ended up as some kind of Christian. Farmer, philosopher, inventor, scientist, and poet, he became by the force of circumstances or some accident of fate a statesman, a soldier, and
finally a bishop. He was elected to the last post, Bishop of Cy-

96

rene, in 409 at a time of crisis not ecclesiastical but political and military when people wanted the kind of leader that the government and the army had failed to provide. For about eight months Synesius deliberated whether to accept the episcopal appointment, then accepted, was baptized, and immediately invested as bishop. He threw himself into his work with energy and enthusiasm; he even excommunicated one obnoxious character who was in fact more deserving of physical rather than spiritual extermination.

One of the literary lights of the fourth century, Synesius produced many poems, was famous for his letters (one hundred and fifty or so have survived), and was also known as an orator and an essayist. His oration *On Kingship* was addressed to the Emperor Arcadius, but although Synesius spent three years at court about the year 400, the bold, chiding tone of his speech makes it doubtful that he delivered his remarks in the royal presence. His experiences in Constantinople also inspired *The Egyptian Tale*, an allegorical account of monkeyshines at the palace. He composed at various times a satire entitled *Eulogy on Baldness*, a philosophic work called *Dion*, a treatise on hunting, and an essay on divination known as *On Dreams*. A firm believer in the prophetic value of dreams, Synesius maintained that divination by dreams must be legal or at least outside the law, because dreaming is involuntary—you simply cannot help it if you dream.

With Synesius we encounter many attitudes already familiar from the Greek Anthology, Libanius, the Cappadocian fathers, the Theodosian Code, and elsewhere. He speaks of the dubious morals of the forum. Lawyers are slippery; officials are corrupt. We have mentioned his faith in divination, and like so many of his contemporaries he had a deep mistrust of the northern barbarians who were then so prominent in the army and at court. Long hair and beards were offensive to him: he said, "There is no long haired man who is not a degenerate or a pervert." Synesius himself was bald, of course—the reason for his *Eulogy on Baldness*. He also professed great admiration for a hairless entertainer who danced on his head, used his cranium for a battering ram, etc., etc.

The home territory, the stamping ground, of Synesius was the so-called Libyan Pentapolis where his family was prominent and owned one or more huge country estates. He could wax as lyrical about Cyrene as Basil or Gregory or Julian about their homelands. Cyrene was noted for its grain, olive oil, and ostriches, and formerly for its silphium, a kind of onion that had once been exported in great quantities. But high taxes had caused the farmers to plow the crop under, and the plant was all but extinct in the fourth century. Ptolemais was the Cyrenaic town with which the family of Synesius was most closely associated, and it was also the seat of Synesius as bishop.

Ptolemais, founded as a Greek *polis* or city state by the Greco-Macedonian rulers of Egypt in the Hellenistic period, was the capital of the Libyan Pentapolis in the fourth century A.D. With a good harbor and an alternative anchorage when the wind blew the wrong way, Ptolemais was a port town and also on the main highway that led along the coast from east to west. Deep wadis on either side of the town and high ground at the south made possible good defences, very necessary in the disturbed conditions of the third, fourth, and fifth centuries A.D.

Ptolemais was excavated by Carl Kraeling and the Oriental Institute in 1956-58,[1] but the finds, although useful and mildly interesting, were not out of the ordinary. A map of the site and its remains dating from 1822 showed the excavators how much deterioration and damage had taken place in just one century. Using this earlier evidence, the records of Italian archaeologists from just before World War II, and their own discoveries, the Americans were able to reconstruct some features of the town and its history. The city plan was recovered. Built on a grid pattern, the principal streets, the *cardines*, were fifty feet wide and ran from north to south; the *decumanus*, the east-west road was twenty-five feet in width. Block-houses were placed on the perimeter of the town, and there was a fortification wall on the south. Two villas of the early Roman period and public baths were found, and there was a huge cistern building necessary because people got their water from wells and stored both well water and rainwater in cisterns. Ptolemais had an amphitheatre, two theaters, and an odeion or music hall—just about par for a Roman town of that size. The odeion with its orchestra (dancing floor) could be converted into a tank for water spectacles, and it was also the place where jugglers and acrobats performed. Moreover, the odeion was probably the scene of the *majuma* dancing and whatever it was they did in the water in connection with it. One gathers that "whatever" was not decent even by the standards of a policeman's benefit program. In 396 Arcadius and Honorius decreed: "It has pleased our Clemency to restore to the provincials the enjoyment of the Majuma, provided, however, that decency, modesty, and chaste manners shall be preserved."[2] Apparently the provisions of the order were not met, because three years later the Augusti changed their minds and said: "We permit the theatrical arts to be practiced, lest, by excessive restriction thereof, sadness may be produced, but we forbid that foul and indecent spectacle which under the name Majuma a shameless license claims for its own."[3] Perhaps the *majuma* should have been mentioned earlier; it seems to have originated in Palestine, and it was very popular in Antioch.

Other finds at Ptolemais included lamps, some coins, the monument of the gladiator Hippomedes, and a great fortress church, a fifth-century structure and symptomatic of the times. The excavators searched in vain for the church of Bishop Synesius, but they were somewhat consoled at finding fragments of a Latin version of Diocletian's Edict of Prices.

To come to Synesius himself, when he was in his early twenties he went to Alexandria in Egypt to complete his education. Alexandria had always been strong in medicine, science, and mathematics and more than adequate in philosophy and literature. By this time, the 390s, the opportunities for instruction in the last two fields were probably as good as and possibly better than in Athens. This was certainly the opinion of Synesius, and he was probably correct, for Libanius, Basil, and Gregory had not been impressed with Athens a generation earlier. We do not hear of goldfish swallowing or marathon bean-bag throwing, but Athens was pretty "collegiate" for the times, and the students, most of them, seem to have got more fun than philosophy out of it. As we have seen previously, the curriculum could hardly be called elective.

Synesius, on the other hand, found his two years in Alexandria immensely stimulating, and what he learned not only stayed with him but he was able to build on it the rest of his life which is, after all, the real test of an education. We are not surprised to learn that there was for Synesius one outstanding teacher at Alexandria, but what is out of the ordinary for that age was that this teacher was a woman: the famous Hypatia who taught geometry, astronomy, and philosophy and found time to publish as well. Her research included a commentary on the *Conic Sections* of Apollonius of Perga and a similar work on the first six books of the *Arithmetica* of Diophantus; she also collaborated with her father in a commentary on Ptolemy's *Syntaxis*. Hypatia gave Synesius a lifelong interest in science and his basic understanding of philosophy, mainly of Plato.

If you were a person not enamored of the orators, or the rhetoricians, or the sophists, or the philosophical magicians like Maximus, but instead wanted good, solid training, Alexandria was the place to go. The giant figure of the second-century Claudius Ptolemy towered over all, but from the time of Diocletian into the fifth century there were other scholars of consequence at Alexandria. The great algebraist Diophantus, a contemporary of Diocletian, begins the list, followed by the geometer Pappus, a contemporary of Constantine, who wrote a history of geometry and produced commentaries on Euclid and Ptolemy. Hypatia's father, Theon, was famous in his own right with his treatise on optics with special reference to mirrors (inspired by the work of Archimedes) and his commentary on the *Almagest* or *Syntaxis* of Ptolemy. Theon and a younger contemporary,

Proclus, head of the Neo-Platonic school at Athens, were honored by an epigram which found its way into the Greek Anthology:

> The book of Theon and Proclus the all-wise. The book exhibits the measurements of the Heavens and the Earth. Theon measures the Heavens and Proclus the Earth, or rather Proclus measures the Earth and Theon the Heavens. Both are worthy of equal praise, and both of them gave and took their respective arguments: for Theon, assuming the learned propositions of Proclus, demonstrates by these the courses of the stars; while Proclus, assuming the demonstrations of Theon, resolves and propounds his positions by their aid. All hail, learned pair.[4]

It is also thought that one of the epigrams of Palladas was addressed to Theon. We know that they were acquainted and possibly close friends. The epigram of Palladas exhorts the intellectuals to humility and reminds us of Basil's letter about the ant. Palladas said:

> Tell me, and wouldst thou span the ends of earth
> Thou tiny body brought from clay to birth?
> Nay, know thyself, and thine own limits see
> Before thou dealest with immensity.
> Count first the dust that does thy body make
> Ere of the measureless thou measure take.[5]

And Basil wrote:

> He who says that the knowledge of all things that really exist is ultimately attainable, by some method and deductive process derived from the knowledge he has already obtained from a study of existences, has set his powers of reasoning to work, and starting from simple and trifling matters, has, so he alleges, trained his faculties of apprehension to that which passeth all understanding.
>
> So let him who boasts that he has apprehended the knowledge of existences, interpret to us the nature of the most diminutive of phenomena. Let him unfold to us the nature of the ant. Doth she live by drawing breath? Is her body constructed upon bones? Are her joints pulled and drawn by sinews and tendons? Is the setting of her sinews controlled by a system of muscles and glands? Doth marrow in her dorsal vertebrae extend from her occiput to her tail? Doth this spinal marrow, by

means of a covering of sinewy membrane, give motive power to her limbs?

Hath she a liver, a gall-bladder beside her liver, kidneys, a heart, arteries and veins, membranes and cartilages? Is she hairy or smooth. Hath she a hoof, or a foot divided into toes? How long liveth she, how long goeth she with young? And why do ants neither all run, nor all fly, but some go upon the ground, others are borne upon the air?

So let him who boasts a knowledge of phenomena, first begin by revealing to us the nature of the ant. Then let him proceed to discourse upon that which passeth all understanding. For if your knowledge is not yet advanced to a comprehension of the smallest thing that goes, how canst thou make it thy boast, that thou hast with thine understanding comprehended the incomprehensible might of God?[6]

The influence of Hypatia on Synesius was lifelong. That he respected, even adored, this brilliant and beautiful woman is apparent in the seven letters that he wrote to her after his student days. Hypatia had many admirers, we are told, but never married. An epigram of Palladas pretty well sums up the reasons for this:

"Revered Hypatia, ornament of learning, stainless star of wise teaching, when I see you and listen to your discourse, I worship you, looking on the starry house of the virgin; for your business is in heaven."[7]

Hypatia was a pagan and because of her prominence almost predestined to become embroiled in the violent quarrels of the Alexandrian Christians who warred upon one another and the pagans as well. Synesius did not live to know the fate of Hypatia, but he could not have condoned the circumstances for which his superior, the bishop of Alexandria, was definitely responsible. The story is a familiar one, if only from Charles Kingsley's novel. Bishop Cyril and the imperial prefect in Egypt, Orestes, had been feuding, and, according to the church historian Socrates, this is what happened:

The regime of Bishop Cyril was a bloody one. His followers had perpetrated a massacre of Jews in a synagogue, and the prefect in retaliation had banished some of the offenders. This put him at odds with Cyril, and before long several hundred armed monks came in from the desert to support the bishop against the prefect. They surrounded the official as he drove through the city in his chariot, insulted him with abusive epithets and called him a pagan though he protested that he had been baptized in Constantinople. Then one monk named Ammonius threw a stone which hit the prefect in the head and drew blood. Ammonius was arrested and publicly tortured. He subsequently died after which Cyril complained to the authorities at Constantinople and proclaimed Ammonius a martyr. The climax came with the murder of Hypatia. Socrates says:

> There was a woman at Alexandria named Hypatia, daughter of the philosopher Theon, who made such attainments in literature and science, as to far surpass all the philosophers of her own time. Having succeeded to the school of Plato and Plotinus, she explained the principles of philosophy to her auditors, many of whom came from a distance to receive her instructions. On account of the self-possession and ease of manner, which she had acquired in consequence of the cultivation of her mind, she not infrequently appeared in public in the presence of the magistrates. Neither did she feel abashed in coming to an assembly of men. For all men on account of her extraordinary dignity and virtue admired her the more. Yet even she fell a victim to the political jealousy which at that time prevailed. For as she had frequent interviews with Orestes, it was calumniously reported among the Christian populace, that it was she who prevented Orestes from being reconciled to the bishop. Some of them therefore, hurried away by a fierce and bigoted zeal, whose ringleader was a reader named Peter, waylaid her returning home, and dragging her from her carriage, they took her to the church called *Caesareum*, where they completely stripped her, and then murdered her with tiles. After tearing her body in pieces, they took her mangled limbs to a place called Cinaron, and there burnt them.[8]

Long before this, having completed two years in Alexandria, Synesius decided to go to school in Athens. He was sceptical about the value of it, but, as he wrote to his brother Evoptius, he had been subjected to so much pressure to study in Athens that he finally capitulated. He would be free of the nagging of his advisors, and he would no longer be treated as an inferior by those who had been to Athens. As he said to Evoptius:

They differ in no wise from us ordinary mortals. They do not understand Aristotle and Plato better than we, and nevertheless they go about
among us as demi-gods among mules, because they have seen the Acade-
my, the Lyceum, and the Painted Porch where Zeno gave his lectures
on philosophy. The Poecile (Painted Porch), however, no longer deserves
its name because the proconsul has taken away all the pictures and thus
humiliated their pretensions to learning.[9]

Athens lived up or down to Synesius' expectations as we
learn from another fraternal letter:

Athens no longer has anything sublime except the country's famous
names. Just as in the case of a victim burnt in the sacrificial fire, there
remains nothing but the skin to help us reconstruct a creature which was
once alive. . . . Today Egypt has received and cherishes the fruitful
wisdom of Hypatia. Athens was once the dwelling place of the wise; today the beekeepers alone bring it honor. It is like that pair of sophists
in Plutarch who draw the young people to the lecture room — not by the
fame of their eloquence, but by pots of honey from Hymettus.[10]

So Synesius came back to Alexandria and from there sailed
home to Cyrene. It may have been on this occasion that he was
shipwrecked. The date is disputed mainly because he mentions
a new moon that made its appearance on a Tuesday, the 18th
of an Egyptian month. Various calculations have suggested the
years 396, 397, 402, 410, and 413 as well as January 28, 404
(Julian calendar); 410 and 413 can pretty well be ruled out.
The two most likely dates are 397 (his return from Athens)
and 402 (when he came back from Constantinople). The youth-
ful buoyant humor of Synesius' letter to his brother describing
the episode leads me to favor 397.

At any rate, he set sail on Friday the 13th for home. The
voyage would take several days. They would normally put in
to shore every night, but this was to be no ordinary voyage.
After they had run aground three times just trying to get out
of the harbor, Synesius had a premonition of worse things to
come. And he was right!

The ship had a Jewish skipper named Amaranthus and a
crew of thirteen most of whom were Egyptian peasants who

had had little experience as sailors and even less as rowers. Every crewman, says Synesius, seemed to have some marked physical defect, and he and some of the other passengers amused themselves by giving each sailor a nickname in accordance with these deformities: Limpy, Lefty, Goggle-eyes, Ruptured, and so on.

There were about fifty passengers, about one-third women "most young and attractive." The sexes were separated by a screen made from a torn sail, but more effective protection for the ladies was soon provided. "Priapus himself," said Synesius, "might well have been temperate if he had sailed with Amaranthus" who almost ran the ship on a reef while under full sail and headed out to sea on a course that would never get them to the Pentapolis. Then the wind changed from a light southern breeze to a violent gale from the north whipping up mountainous waves that threatened to capsize the vessel. Amaranthus promised to head in for shore but delayed changing his course. The storm worsened, and about sunset to the consternation of everyone Amaranthus left the helm to begin his Friday preparation for the Sabbath by sitting down to read his roll. The passengers pleaded with the skipper to no avail. One of the soldiers on board even threatened him with his sword, but nothing could disturb the devotions of the pious Amaranthus.

It was past midnight before Amaranthus finally acknowledged that the ship was in grave danger and resumed his post at the helm. Since the ship was running under full sail with ropes and pulleys hopelessly tangled the plight of crew and passengers seemed desperate indeed. As many of the sepulchral epigrams of the Greek Anthology attest, the people of classical antiquity regarded death by drowning the worst fate of all. Synesius noticed that many of the soldiers had drawn their weapons in the determination to kill themselves rather than surrender to the briny deep, while other passengers were fastening bags of money or objects of jewelry about their necks so that Charon's fee would be provided for anyone who found their bodies washed up on shore and thus ensure for them a decent burial.

By morning the sea was calmer, however, and they were able to make a landing. They felt at first that all their troubles were over but soon discovered that the area was desert for miles around and they must put out to sea again. More storms followed. When a safe harbor was found at last, their vessel was joined by nearly a dozen others also seeking refuge. Marooned for a week and faced with starvation, they would have perished had they not been befriended by natives who brought them food. Days later they came finally to the Pentapolis.

Synesius ends this long letter to his brother with the words, "As for you, may you never trust yourself to the sea or at least if you really must do so, let it not be at the end of the month." Combined with another remark made earlier in the letter, we have enough to assure us that Synesius, like his contemporaries, was a firm believer in astrology and lucky and unlucky days, for he has already said, "It was the thirteenth day of the waning moon, and a great danger was now impending, I mean the conjunction of certain constellations and those well known chance events which no one, they say, ever confronted at sea with impunity."[11]

The carefree days of youth were now over. About 399 Synesius went as the emissary of his province, Cyrene, to Constantinople to acquaint the Emperor Arcadius with the desperate situation of the people in the Pentapolis plagued as they were by locusts, hostile Libyan tribes, and maladministration by imperial officials. The embassy took three years. Synesius could not get an audience with the emperor for a long time. It was not merely a matter of bureaucratic red tape—which might have delayed him only for two years—but rather because there were other matters more pressing that engaged the indolent Arcadius in spite of himself.

Affairs at Constantinople were indeed in a tangled state. Alaric had threatened the Balkans. The once mighty eunuch Eutropius had fallen from power because of resentment over his election to the consulate. Protected by John Chrysostom, the patriarch, Eutropius had only been deposed instead of executed, but Chrysostom had troubles of his own and would shortly lose his own job after calling the empress a Jezebel. Parenthetically, John Chrysostom had come a long way since the days of Libanius, Valens, and the Riot of the Statues, but he had made enemies, among them Theophilus, bishop of Alexandria, who would ultimately be the superior of Synesius.

Nevertheless, one of the chief enemies of Eutropius, Chrysostom, and just about everyone else as it turned out was the Goth, Gainas, the trusted general of Arcadius who was as false to his trust as his contemporary Stilicho was loyal to his. A rebellion of Ostrogothic colonists in Anatolia had occurred. Gainas for reasons of his own allowed this uprising to attain dangerous proportions. The new praetorian prefect, Aurelian, a strong anti-barbarian in sentiment, was surrendered as a hostage as Gainas and the Goths marched on the capital. Dominating Constantinople for six months, Gainas and his Goths finally marched away northward in midsummer of 400 and were subsequently chased out of Roman territory by a loyal Gothic admiral. Later, the Huns caught Gainas and sent his head to Arcadius as a Christmas present. Aurelian was returned to power, and an anti-barbarian reaction began in earnest.

Now, since Synesius was intimate with Aurelian, we may suspect that his oration on kingship was composed after 400. The burden of Synesius' advice to Arcadius was that an emperor ought to lead his own troops instead of lurking in the palace, that the barbarians must be dismissed and a citizen army recruited in their place, and that the soldiers should be made to treat civilians with respect—not to act like dogs who chase away the wolf so that they themselves may prey upon the flock. It was all pretty strong stuff, and it seems very likely that Synesius' tract was privately circulated and perhaps not even written until he was safely back home.

In 402 there was an earthquake in Constantinople. Synesius left the capital on the earliest departing vessel without saying good-bye to any of his fine friends. Back home, he got married, produced three sons none of whom survived childhood, and may even have divorced his wife when he became bishop in 409 although this is, in my opinion, extremely doubtful because of passages in two of Synesius' letters. In the first he says, "God himself, the law of the land, and the blessed hand of Theophilus himself have given me a wife. I therefore proclaim to all and call them to witness that I will not be separated from her, nor shall I associate with her surreptitiously like an adulterer — I shall desire and pray to have many virtuous children. This is what I must inform this man (Theophilus) upon whom depends my consecration."[12] And again, in the midst of warfare against the marauding Libyans, he wrote, "If I am called upon to die, here lies the advantage of philosophy, not to regard it as a terrible thing to retire from this poor envelope of the flesh. But whether I shall be tearless in the presence of my wife and child, of this I dare give no pledge; would that philosophy were so powerful. But may I never have to make trial of her. Never, O saviour, O guardian of freedom!"[13]

At home in Cyrene there was now continuous warfare against the marauders with Synesius leading the defense for lack of any governmental support. The authorities did not want the populace armed, but Synesius constructed catapults and supervised the manufacture of weapons. "I have already 300 lances and as many scimitars. As for two-edged swords I never had more than ten for they do not manufacture these very long weapons in our country. I think that scimitars strike the bodies of our enemies a more terrible blow, and we shall use them for that reason. At a pinch we can have clubs, for our wild olive trees are excellent. Some of our men also carry hatchets."[14]

Naturally, Synesius was elected bishop. There was no imperial authority that people could turn to, and they hoped that God would increase the strength of their one champion. As bishop, therefore, Synesius had to continue as general. By this time he had the dubious assistance of one Joannes, a real Miles Gloriosus if there ever was one. Joannes became the bane of Synesius' existence. On one memorable occasion, after Joannes had assured everyone that the enemy was afraid of his very

name, they encountered a small raiding party of the foe. The
following passage will suffice to delineate the military excellence of Joannes:

> The moment that they saw us, as we also saw them, before they were
> within javelin throw, they jumped from their horses, as is their way, to
> give battle on foot. I was of the opinion that we ought to do the same
> thing, for the ground did not lend itself to cavalry manoeuvres. But our
> noble friend said that he would not renounce the arts of horsemanship,
> and insisted on delivering a cavalry attack. What then? He pulls the horse's
> head sharply to the side, turns and flees away at full gallop, covers his
> horse with blood, gives it full rein, incites it with frequent application
> of spear, whip, and voice. I really do not know which of the two to ad-
> mire the more, the horse or the rider, for if the horse galloped up hill
> and down hill and over rough country and smooth alike, cleared ditches
> and banks at a bound, the horseman for his part, kept his seat in the saddle
> firm and unshaken. I am sure the enemy thought it a fine sight, and were
> anxious to have many such. We could not give them this satisfaction,
> but you may imagine that we were disconcerted after having taken the
> promises of this hirsute beauty so seriously.[15]

There was no engagement, as it turned out. Both sides withdrew in good order. As for Joannes, he took refuge in a mountain honeycombed with caves "like a field mouse in its hole"
and did not emerge until all danger was past.

Even so Joannes hung on and even gained new support from
the imperial appointment of an administrator named Chilas of
whom Synesius remarked: "You remember Chilas, I suppose;
I mean the one who kept a disorderly house. Probably few do
not know him. He was quite celebrated in his walk of life. Andromache, the actress, who was one of the prettiest women of
our time, was part of his company. After having passed his
youth in this honorable career, he took it into his head that it
would be a fitting sequel to his honorable career to shine in
his old age by military achievements. . . . Our wonderful
Joannes in a word is in the same position as ever."[16]

These were not all the troubles of Synesius. He had to cope
with Andronicus, an imperial jackal who refused to admit to

the church the right of sanctuary. At last, Synesius excommunicated Andronicus. In a letter to the bishops on this subject, Synesius pronounced the fateful sentence:

> Let the precincts of no house of God be open to Andronicus and his associates. . . . Let every holy sanctuary and enclosure be shut in their faces. There is no part in Paradise for the Devil: even if he has secretly crept in, he is cast out. I exhort, therefore, every private individual and ruler not to be under the same roof, nor to be seated at the same table, particularly priests, for these shall neither speak to him while living, nor join in his funeral procession, when dead.[17]

Synesius was later inclined to forgive the repentant Andronicus, but that is another story as is much more that might be said of Synesius the bishop, Synesius the poet, Synesius the scientist, and so on.

Synesius was not forty-five when he died, and near the end he wrote to his beloved goddess, Hypatia:

> I am dictating this letter to you from my bed, but may you receive it in good health, mother, sister, teacher, benefactress, and whatever else is honored in name and deed. For me bodily weakness has followed in the wake of mental suffering. The remembrance of my departed children is consuming my forces little by little. Only so long should Synesius have lived as he was still without experience of the evils of life. It is as if a torrent long pent up had burst upon me in full volume and as if the sweetness of life had vanished. May I either cease to live or cease to think of the tomb of my sons. But may you preserve your health and give my salutations to your happy comrades in turn.[18]

This is the last of his surviving letters, and it may have been the last he ever wrote. It was a sad end for one so full of life, who enjoyed living to the fullest, and who had so much more to give.

CHAPTER VIII

The Roman

Like the Pilgrim of 333, after traveling through the Empire, we come at last to Rome and shall return to Milan and Gaul. Although it was no longer the capital of the empire, many roads still led to Rome, and in the last quarter of the fourth century A.D. Rome was either the residence of or a place of sojourn for many well-known persons some of whom we have already met: Ausonius, Ammianus, Claudian, and Jerome, for example. St. Augustine and St. Ambrose were to live in Rome and later go to Milan. The great pagan Symmachus, like a proper Bostonian, had no need to travel, for Rome was his ancestral locus.

As yet ravaged neither by time or by barbarians, Rome had lost none of its imperial grandeur, only its emperors, and even they, being mortal, were humbled by its eternity and splendor when they came to visit, for they often went about gaping like ordinary tourists. The famous passage in Ammianus describing the entrance of Constantius II into Rome and his subsequent sightseeing really says it all:

> Accordingly, being saluted as Augustus with favoring shouts, while hills and shores thundered out the roar, he never stirred, but showed himself as calm and unperturbable as he was commonly seen in his provinces. For he both stooped when passing through lofty gates (although he was very short), and as if his neck were in a vise, he kept the gaze of his eyes

straight ahead, and turned his face neither to right nor to left, but neither did he nod when the wheel jolted nor was he ever seen to spit, or to wipe or rub his face or nose, or move his hands about. . . . So he entered Rome . . . and when he had come to the Rostra, the most renowned forum of ancient dominion, he stood amazed; and on every side on which his eyes rested he was dazzled by the array of marvelous sights . . . As he surveyed the sections of the city and its suburbs . . . he thought that whatever first met his gaze towered above all the rest: the sanctuaries of Tarpeian Jove; the baths built up to the measure of provinces; the huge bulk of the amphitheatre (Coliseum) . . . to whose top eyesight barely ascends; the Pantheon like a rounded city district, vaulted over in lofty beauty . . . the Forum of Peace, the Theatre of Pompey. . . . But when he came to the Forum of Trajan, a construction unique under the heavens . . . he stood fast in wonder, turning his attention to the gigantic complex about him, beggaring description and never again to be imitated by mortal men. . . . When the emperor had viewed many objects with awe and amazement, he complained of Fame as either incapable or spiteful, because while always exaggerating everything, in describing what there is in Rome, she becomes shabby.[1]

For pious Christians, there were other marvels just as exciting as the pagan monuments: three splendid churches erected by Constantine—the Lateran Basilica, the Basilica of St. Peter with its Tomb of the Fisherman, and the smaller church covering the tomb of the Apostle Paul. One also visited the Sessorian Basilica to see the portion of the True Cross discovered by St. Helena, and then there were many tombs of the martyrs and finally the catacombs to be explored. St. Jerome remembered all this:

When I was a boy at Rome and was being educated in liberal studies, I was accustomed with others of like age and mind to visit on Sundays the sepulchres of the apostles and martyrs. And often did I enter the crypts deep dug in the earth with their walls on either side lined with the bodies of the dead where everything is so dark that it almost seems as if the psalmist's words were fulfilled, "Let them go down quick into hell." Here and there the light not entering in through windows but filtering down from above through shafts relieves the horror of the darkness.[2]

Jerome and Ammianus have more to tell us about Rome, not so much about the city but rather about its inhabitants, or better yet, denizens. We shall deal with the remarks of each in turn, but each of these authors also deserves a biographical sketch since both are representative of their age.

Ammianus, the only notable Latin historian after Tacitus, was actually a Greek from Antioch born about 330 A.D. A veteran of fifteen years off and on in the Roman army, Ammianus fought in the Near East against Shapur in the fifties, had a tour of duty in the West where he first saw Julian, and then later participated in Julian's last and fatal campaign against the Persians in 363. After going home to Antioch for a time, Ammianus migrated to Rome in 378 where he lived until his death in the nineties.

This is not the time or the place to discuss the complex and mysterious matter of Amminaus' historical compositions. Of the thirty-one books of his history, the first thirteen are lost, and it is clear that Books 26-31 which cover the period 364-78 were added to an original work (Books 1-25) at a late date. But did Ammianus deal with the whole time span from the accession of Nerva in 96 to the death of Jovian in 364 in those first twenty-five books? If he did, the work lacked balance because the surviving Books 14-25 cover only eleven years, an average of slightly over one book per year. Or did he start with the death of Constantine in 337 so that the missing Books 1-13 related the events of sixteen years? And if so, did he first write an epitome of Roman history in the fashion of Victor and Eutropius? Victor ended his brief work with Constantius, and Eutropius by a remarkable coincidence stopped like Ammianus in Book 25 with the death of Jovian.

Why Ammianus, a Greek, should write in Latin is not so much a mystery. It was the fashion. Victor, who does not seem at home in the language, Eutropius, Festus, the Anonymous Valesianus, and the equally anonymous author of the *Epitome de Caesaribus* all wrote in Latin in this period, not to mention the author or authors of the *Augustan History* whose work, in my opinion, also should be assigned to the third quarter of the fourth century.

Opinion is divided about Ammianus' Latin style, but no one disputes his value as an historical source for his age, and his great narrative passages are justly famous. Ammianus has a kind of split personality: he has difficulty deciding whether he is an old soldier with the usual contempt for civilians, or whether he is an educated Greek who must parade his learning. He is at his best in his military role; when he wears his other hat he treats us to long digressions on subjects that even we know better than he does, or he gets carried away by his rhetoric and overstates his case. We have to keep this in mind when we read his characterization of the Romans which is a little florid, and we also have to remember that as a non-Roman it took him some time before he got the kind of acceptance in Rome that he thought he deserved. If his testimony were not supported in many details by that of Jerome we should be suspicious indeed. Ammianus is particularly critical of the upper-class Romans with their idle vanities, pretentiousness, and consuming interests in matters of no importance. It may be revealing of his own experiences and disappointments at Rome when he says, "Some of them hate learning as they do poison, and read with attentive care only Juvenal and Marius Maximus,"[3] or:

> If as a stranger of good position you enter for the first time to pay your respects to some man who is rich and therefore puffed up, at first you will be greeted as if you were an eagerly expected friend, and . . . you will wonder, since the man never saw you before, that a great personage should pay such marked attention to your humble self as to make you regret that, because of such special kindness, you did not see Rome ten years earlier. When encouraged by this affability, you make the same call on the following day, you will hang about unknown and unexpected, while the man who the day before urged you to call again counts up his clients, wondering who you are and whence you came.[4]

Ammianus has even less regard for the "idle and slothful commons" with their drunkenness, addiction to gambling, and generally worthless pursuits. He says:

Their temple, their assembly, their dwelling, and the height of all their hopes is the Circus Maximus. . . . Among them those who have enjoyed a surfeit of life, influential through long experience, often swear by their hoary hair and wrinkles that the state cannot exist if in the coming race the charioteer whom each favors is not the first to rush forth from the barriers, and fails to round the turning point closely with his ill-omened horses. . . . If from there they come to worthless theatrical pieces, any actor is hissed off the boards who has not won the favour of the low rabble with money.[5]

He goes on to speak of the claque, that applauds actors and other entertainers, conveniently forgetting the influence of the claque in Antioch, and he is also critical of the dependence of all Romans on astrology—as if that were confined to Rome in his age. Naturally, too, he has a low opinion of lawyers, both advocates and jurisconsults, although he admits that this plague is not a Roman disease but rampant empire-wide.

And finally:

We have reached such a state of baseness that . . . when there was fear of a scarcity of food, foreigners were driven neck and crop from the city, and those who practised the liberal arts (very few in number), were thrust out without breathing space, yet the genuine attendants upon actresses of the mimes, and those who for the time pretend to be such, were kept with us, while three thousand dancing girls, without even being questioned, remained here with their choruses, and an equal number of dancing masters.[6]

Turning now to Jerome we shall see that his strictures on the Romans are equally severe and somewhat parallel to the remarks of Ammianus, but it is perhaps well to remember that the weight of this dual evidence is somewhat lightened by the fact that both Ammianus and Jerome, for different reasons, felt that the Romans had not treated them as well as they deserved.

Jerome was born near Aquileia about 340 A.D. He was a student in Rome in the sixties where he learned his rhetoric well. During this same period, Damasus, Jerome's future superior and benefactor, became Pope after a bloody election involving the Arian and Orthodox factions each of which, of course, had a candidate. According to Ammianus:

> Damasus and Ursinus, burning with a superhuman desire of seizing the bishopric, engaged in bitter strife, because of the opposing interests; and the supporters of both parties went even so far as conflicts ending in bloodshed and death. Since Viventius (the city prefect) was able neither to end nor to diminish this strife, he was compelled to yield to its great violence, and retired to the suburbs. And in the struggle Damasus was victorious through the efforts of the party which favored him. It is a well-known fact that in the basilica of Sicininus, where the assembly of the Christian sect is held, in a single day a hundred and thirty-seven corpses of the slain were found, and that it was only with difficulty that the long continued frenzy of the people was afterwards quieted.[7]

After completing his schooling in Rome, Jerome went back to Aquileia where with his half-brother and a few friends he conceived the idea of embracing the monastic life and founding their own community—just like Basil and Gregory. This venture was of short duration, and eventually Jerome headed for the East where he visited Antioch and went to Constantinople in the late seventies where he made the acquaintance of Gregory of Nazianzus. After the council at which Gregory resigned his post and his chances of election to the patriarchate, Jerome was invited by Pope Damasus, who had attended the council, to come back to Rome as a papal secretary. Jerome accepted and became the ghost writer for Damasus. He later boasted, "Damasus was my mouth." Perhaps Jerome even composed the several epitaphs bearing the name of Damasus which have survived, including the one for Damasus supposedly authored by Damasus himself. It reads:

> He who stilled the fierce waves of the sea by walking thereon;
> He who make the dying seeds of the earth to live;
> He who could loose for Lazarus his chains of death and
> Give back to the world above her brother to his sister Martha,
> After three days and nights,
> He, I believe, will make me, Damasus, arise from my ashes.[8]

It was Damasus who set Jerome to collecting, collating, and improving the text of the Latin Bible which existed in several different and regional versions at that time. In this kind of scholarly endeavor Jerome was at his best. He translated from the Greek of the New Testament and learned Hebrew so that he could turn the Old Testament, too, into Latin.

It was also during the period 382-85 when Jerome was serving Damasus that he became the darling of the Christian society ladies in Rome including, of course, the holy Paula. Toxotius, Paula's husband, after fathering four daughters and a son, had given up the ghost leaving Paula a widow at thirty-five. It should not surprise anyone that the bereaved Paula soon drifted into the orbit of Jerome. Then the fun began:

Blesilla, one of Paula's daughters, had already been widowed at the age of twenty and had plunged into the lively social life of Rome to forget her misfortune. But after a serious illness from which recovery appeared miraculous and the result of divine intervention, she renounced the world to become an ascetic. This pleased her mother and also Jerome, who trumpeted, "God has permitted Blesilla to be tormented for thirty days in order to teach her not to pamper a body that is soon to become food for worms." The wormy part came sooner than anticipated, for Blesilla died in 384, and the story began to circulate in Rome that her mother and her spiritual advisor had hastened the end by forcing her into fasting and other austerities.

These stories soon led to others about the relationship between Paula and Jerome. To be charitable, we must assume that all this was pure gossip, but some people—and there were more than some—who did not like Jerome were only too willing to believe the worst. Always cantankerous, loud, and contentious, Jerome had made enemies in many quarters with his criticisms of the Romans in general, Roman ladies who did not choose to join his society sewing circle, and the Roman clergy. In December 384 Pope Damasus died, and Jerome was passed over as his successor. Embattled and embittered, Jerome left the eternal city never to return. Paula soon followed him. They met in Antioch and proceeded to the Holy Land. He settled in Bethlehem where, as we already know, Paula came to rest. She and Eustochium died in Bethlehem, and so did he.

A little bit of Jerome on the warpath against the Romans will go a long way. In an open letter to Eustochium he said of Roman ladies:

> It is not only that I wish you to decline the company of those who are puffed up with their husbands' dignities, who are hedged in by a crowd of eunuchs, who wear cloth of gold, but avoid also those whom necessity has made widows; not that they ought to have desired the death of their husbands, but that when they had the opportunity of living a continent life, they did not embrace it of their own good will. They have changed their habit, but not their desires. A troop of eunuchs and servants surrounds their litters, and from their rosy cheeks and plump persons you would suppose they were seeking husbands rather than that they had lost them. Their houses are crowded with flatterers and feasters. The clergy themselves, who ought to maintain the reverence due their office and the deference due to their guidance, kiss their foreheads and stretch forth their hands—you would think it was to give a benediction if you did not know it was to receive a present.[9]

Or again to Eustochium:

> Do not, now you have ceased to pride yourself in golden robes, begin to take pride in shabby ones; do not, when you come into a meeting of brethren, or of sisters, go and seat yourself in the lowest place. Do not speak in a faint voice, as if you were half dead with fasting, and affect a feeble gait, and lean upon somebody's shoulder. For there are some who "disfigure their faces, and appear unto men to fast," who when they see anyone coming begin to groan, cast down their eyes, and cover their faces, so that they hardly leave an eye to see with. Their robe is brown, and their girdle of leather, and their feet and hands soiled, only their stomach, which nobody can see into, is filled with food. . . . There are others who are ashamed to be women as they were born; they wear men's clothes, cut their hair short, and walk about shamelessly, looking like eunuchs. And still others, who affect the simplicity and innocence of infancy, dress themselves in elaborate hoods, and make themselves look like owls.

But lest I should seem to find fault with women only; avoid those men whom you see wearing iron chains, with their hair long, like women, contrary to the command of the Apostle, with a goat's beard, a black cloak, and bare feet, pinched with cold. These things are all tokens of the devil. Rome, a while ago, had to complain of such a one as Antimus, and more recently Sophronius, men who gain entrance into the houses of the nobles, and deceive silly women, laden with sins, always learning, and never coming to the knowledge of truth, who affect gravity, and make long fasts, by taking food secretly at night. . . . There are others who take the priesthood and deaconate for bad purposes. All their anxiety is about their dress, whether they are well perfumed, whether their shoes of soft leather fit without a wrinkle. Their hair is curled with tongs, their fingers glitter with rings, and they walk tip-a-toe, lest the wet road should soil the soles of their shoes. When you see them you would take them for bridegrooms rather than clerics; whose whole thought and life it is to know the names, and houses, and doings of the rich ladies. One of these men, who is the prince of this art, I will briefly and concisely describe for you, in order that when you know the master you may the more readily recognize his disciples. He hastes to rise with the sun, he arranges the order of his visits, he seeks short cuts, and the troublesome old man almost pushes his way into the bedchambers of people before they are awake. If he happens to see a cushion, a pretty napkin, or a piece of furniture, he praises it, he admires it, he handles it, he complains that he lacks such things; and he not so much begs it, as extorts it: for everyone fears to offend the city newsman. Chastity he hates, fasting he hates; what he likes is the smell of dinner, and his weakness is—suckling pig. He has a barbarous and forward tongue, always ready for bad language. Wherever you go, there he is. Whatever news you hear, he is either the author or the exaggerator of it.[10]

The truly high society of Rome was perhaps decadent but certainly not as immoral or unprincipled as Ammianus and Jerome alleged. Mostly this enclave was composed of aristocratic pagans, and it constituted an in-group to which admittance would be denied a Jerome or an Ammianus. Remote as the Olympians they worshiped, largely insulated from the rest of the world, formal and correct to the point of stuffiness, they were the last of their kind, antediluvian to the Christian flood, and doomed to extinction. Our knowledge of them comes in large part from the letters of Symmachus and the writings of that pseudo-scientist Macrobius.

Symmachus, the pagan champion who entered the lists against the Christians, was born in the early forties and died in 402 or 403 — probably before he could be wounded by the *Contra Symmachum*, the two poems by Prudentius attacking him. An acknowledged master of oratory, rhetoric, and epistolography — the main reason for the survival of his writings — we know Symmachus from a dozen orations and some 900 letters including 49 *relationes*, reports to the emperor when Symmachus was Prefect of the City (Rome). The cursus, the career, of Symmachus is summarized in an inscription (*CIL* VI 1699) erected by his son and found on the Caelian Hill in Rome. It reads:

> To Quintus Aurelius Symmachus, vir clarissimus, quaestor, praetor, pontifex maior, corrector of Lucania and the Brutii, count of the third order, proconsul of Africa, prefect of the city, consul ordinarius, a most eloquent orator (erected by) Q. Fabius Memmius Symmachus, vir clarissimus, to the best of fathers.[11]

Symmachus, who owed his wealth and his start in public life to his father, Avianus, a distinguished senator, was proconsul in Africa in 373-74 where he cooperated with Theodosius, father of the future emperor, in putting down a revolt. He was city prefect in 384 and held the consulship more than once, but his term as consul ordinarius was in 391. Between the holding of the high offices already mentioned, the prominence of Symmachus was sustained by the fact that he had succeeded his father as *princeps senatus*, really spokesman of the Senate, in 376.

As a source for the march of events in this period the letters of Symmachus are very disappointing. They are a mine of information about his literary, social, and family life, but there is little reference to imperial politics, internal disturbances, or barbarian invasions. It was probably not that Symmachus fiddled while Rome burned, but rather that, as we know, his correspondence was edited and published by his son who, like any member of a family even now, would see to it that anything damaging to his father's reputation or to his own career would be suppressed—and his father had been dangerously involved on the wrong side in both the usurpation of Maximus and that of Eugenius. In all fairness to the younger Symmachus, however, it should be stated that most of the letters in the collection were those that Symmachus himself intended for publication. During his lifetime he had complained that his letters were being pirated and sold in Rome, but since in many cases when he wrote to one person he appended copies to be distributed to selected friends, it was not that Symmachus objected to the circulation, but he was afraid that corrupt copies might damage his reputation as a stylist.

A good sample of Symmachus as a letter writer is provided by his exchange with Ausonius. You remember Ausonius, the grammaticus and poet of Bordeaux, who had risen from the ranks to be the tutor of Gratian, then prefect of Gaul, and at last consul in 378. Again, a little bit will go a long way:

Symmachus to Ausonius

Your learned pages, which I received while staying at Capua, brought me sheer delight. For there was in them a certain gaiety overlaid with honey from Tully's (Cicero's) hive, and some eulogy on my discourse, flattering rather than deserved. And so I am at a loss to decide which to admire the more—the graces of your diction or of your disposition. Indeed you so far surpass all others in eloquence that I fear to write in reply; you so generously approve my essays that I am glad to keep silence. . . . But in this I think you are excessively modest, that you complain of me for playing traitor to your book. For it is easier to hold hot coals in one's mouth than to keep the secret of a brilliant work. Once you have let a poem out of your hands, you have renounced all your rights: a speech delivered is common property . . . etc., etc.

Ausonius to Symmachus

Now I understand how honey-sweet is the power of speech, how enchanting and persuasive a thing is eloquence! You have made me believe that my letter delivered to you at Capua was not a barbarous compilation; but this only for so long as I am actually reading your letter, which is so spread, as it were, with the syrup of your nectar as to overpersuade me while I hang agape over its allurements . . . etc., etc.[12]

As the spokesman of the Senate and as pontifex maior, Symmachus led the last ditch fight of paganism in Rome. It was typical of his really untenable position, however, that he had thunder but no lightning. When one of the Vestal Virgins turned out to be more Vestal than anything else, he could not have her thrown off the Tarpeian Rock, as of old, but had to turn her over to the civil authorities who were not too anxious to catch that hot potato, either.

The most valiant and best known of the efforts of Symmachus on behalf of paganism were connected with the affair of the Altar and Statue of Victory which had been ordered to be removed from the Senate House. The pious Gratian had renewed the dormant order of Constantius relating to this matter and even worse commanded that state support of pagan sacrifices and ceremonies be terminated, that landed property willed to pagan priests be confiscated to the treasury, and that pagan religious officials could no longer receive bequests of land. What it all came down to was that the Altar and Statue of Victory were merely symbols of surviving paganism. Gratian would not even discuss any relaxation of his orders, but he was assassinated in 383 and pagan hopes rose as Valentinian II gave the appearance of being more friendly than his half-brother. In 384 as Prefect of the City Symmachus presented his famous *relatio de ara Victoriae* to the emperor. As he pleads for equal rights with the Christians, Symmachus uses arguments that they, the Christians, had once used when the positions had been reversed. "It is just," says Symmachus, "that all worship should be considered as one. We look upon the same stars, the sky is common, the same world surrounds us. What difference does it make by what religious system each seeks the truth? It is impossible by one single path to attain to such a great mystery."[13]

The effort failed this time and yet again in 391, largely because of the counterattack launched by Ambrose, the militant bishop of Milan, to whose life and work we now turn.

One can hardly talk about the late fourth century in the West without mentioning Ambrose. Born in Trier in 339 where his father was praetorian prefect of the Gauls—all western Europe north of the Alps—Ambrose had every advantage of birth and position necessary to ensure a brilliant career in the imperial service. Even though his father died early, Ambrose was educated in Rome, trained in rhetoric, and soon became a lawyer serving as an advocate on the staff of the governor of the upper Danube at Sirmium. After this Ambrose went on to become a governor himself; with headquarters at Milan his province was northern Italy. At that time the bishop of Milan was an Arian, although he managed to get along with the pre-dominantly Orthodox population there. When the bishop died in 373, however, a struggle ensued. Ambrose went to the cathedral where the election of a new bishop was being discussed with Arian and Catholics each determined to have the victory. Instead of calming the disturbance, Ambrose found himself in the middle of it, and when a child's voice was heard crying "Ambrose Bishop!" he was spontaneously and unanimously chosen to serve. Ambrose did not want to be a bishop; he had not even been baptized. Several times he tried to escape from the city, but he was apprehended, taken into custody, and forced to submit to the people's will. On December 1, 373, he was consecrated. The whole matter was in violation of every rule and canon, but no one raised any objection.

Like Synesius in Cyrene, Ambrose took his new job very seriously; but unlike Synesius he dared to face down imperial opposition, even that of the emperor himself. His first contest came with Justina, the mother of Valentinian II, who was determined to have a separate Arian basilica in Milan. Ambrose resisted, saying to the emperor, "We render unto Caesar what is Caesar's, but the churches belong to the bishop." He won!

In the next year after the contest with Justina (386) Ambrose dedicated a basilica of his own. There was a demand that the structure should be consecrated by a deposit of relics of the martyrs within it. Ambrose agreed to this with the reservation

that genuine relics must be found. Excavations were then con-
ducted in a place reputedly sanctified by the bones of martyrs,
and the skeletons of two gigantic males were dug up; they were
headless and covered with a reddish substance that was assumed
to be blood. So the bones of St. Gervasius and St. Protasius
were interred in the new basilica, and when he died in 397 Ambrose was buried with them in a silver casket. Modern opinion
has it that Ambrose in his digging struck a prehistoric cemetery
belonging to people who customarily decapitated their dead
and painted their bones with ochre. If that is so, then some-
where in the great beyond there are two large headless horse-
men who either believe in the transmigration of souls or are
giving Ambrose the horse laugh.

Right or wrong, Ambrose was a fighter. He talked Theodosius out of forcing the Christians to pay for a synagogue
that they had destroyed in the East, and then as something
of an encore he threatened the emperor with excommunica-
tion unless he did penance for the massacre of 7,000 people
at Thessalonica following an anti-imperial riot in that city.
Theodosius knuckled under but was less than grateful to Ambrose for the chastisement. At this point (391) the pagans in
Rome thought it a good time to send Symmachus to renew
the request to restore the Altar of Victory at the Senate House.
Theodosius, badgered by Ambrose not to accede, was mad at
everybody, and the appearance of Symmachus to plead for
the opposite course was the straw that broke the camel's back.
The distinguished consul ordinarius, *princeps senatus*, and
paragon of the pagans was bundled into an uncushioned post
wagon and hustled off to the hundredth milestone beyond
Milan. That was the end of that. The pagans had lost, Ambrose
had won again; and Symmachus was ailing and in semiretire-
ment for the remaining years of his life.

New light on the past does not come solely from discoveries
of new material, but often our own experience of the changing

present permits us to see antiquity in a different perspective. Again, a new arrangement of old material can lead to a new understanding. By way of conclusion, therefore, let me give you a small sample of this:

It was in my original plan not to deal with St. Augustine in these chapters. It seemed to me that he could use a little rest from the prying and prodding to which the poor fellow has been subjected over the ages. But in rereading the *Confessions* the other evening I saw this work not as the unique experience of one man but rather as the epitome of everything we have been saying about the common denominators of the Fourth Century.

Augustine was born in 354, about the time that Abinnaeus passes from our view, and he outlived most of the other people we have been talking about for he died in 430. But Augustine knew Symmachus, who got him his job teaching rhetoric at Milan where he would meet Ambrose who would start him on the road toward conversion. He did not encounter Jerome face to face, but the two got into a theological dispute later on, and Augustine, who started the fight, was treated to some of Jerome's acrimonious letters. One might even say that getting into an argument with Jerome was one of the common denominators of our period just like becoming a bishop as Augustine also did. Unlike Napoleon's soldiers, each of whom was said to carry a marshal's baton in his knapsack, a bishop's mitre was practically always to be found among the impedimenta of our Fourth Century friends.

Trained in and a teacher of rhetoric to begin with, Augustine had the same background for potential leadership as Basil, the Gregories, Libanius, Synesius, and Ambrose. Like many, he came late to Christianity and first traveled other roads in his search for some real meaning in life. He tried Greek philosophy, then Manichaeanism, then Neo-Platonism, each of which brought him closer to his final destination. At last he came to rest in the harbor of Christianity but not without some difficulty in getting over the reefs and shoals. The simplicity and more than that the literary deficiencies of the synoptic gospels put him off. In Milan he went often to hear Ambrose preach. Though he admired Ambrose as a scholar, what Ambrose said seemed unimportant; but his style was worth the price of admission as far as Augustine was concerned. In the end it was St. Paul who spoke to Augustine in a language he could both appreciate and understand. St. Paul aroused his interest in a way that the others could not. Augustine did not have the theological and traditional background to comprehend Ambrose, but Paul began with first principles as every missionary should. At last, Augustine was ready for conversion, but how did it happen? He heard a voice chanting, "Take up and read! Take up and read!" In his own words, "There I had laid the volume of the Apostle. . . . I seized, I opened, and in silence read that section on which my eyes first fell." It was *Romans* XIII.13-14: "Not in rioting and drunkenness, not in chambering and wantonness, not in strife and envying, but put on the Lord Jesus Christ and make not provision for the flesh to fulfill the lusts thereof." And Augustine says, "No further would I read, nor did I need to . . . for instantly all the darkness of doubt had vanished."

Before all this Augustine had lived the boisterous life of a student; he believed in astrology and had consulted an astrologer; he had come to hate lawyers and corrupt officials, he had consulted with friends about organizing an ascetic commune. Like Libanius, he loved the stage, and like Libanius, he never married, but had a son of whom he was very fond. Afterward, like Gregory Nazianzus, he was to be made a priest under duress. Like Gregory, Basil, and Libanius, he was devoted to his mother. Monnica was a Christian, and her fondest hope, ultimately realized, was that Augustine would join her in the faith.

Moreover, it is through Monnica that we finally come to understand why Gregory Nazianzus included with his epigrams on grave robbers several others condemning "those who feast in the churches of the martyrs." According to Augustine,

When my mother had once (in Milan) as was the custom in Africa, brought to the churches built in memory of the saints, certain cakes and bread and wine, and was forbidden by the doorkeeper; so soon as she knew the bishop (Ambrose) had forbidden this, she piously and obediently embraced his wishes. . . . For wine-bibbing did not lay siege to her spirit (Augustine has conveniently forgotten that Monnica had a brush with alcoholism at a tender age), nor did love of wine provoke her to hatred of the truth as it does too many both men and women who revolt at a lesson in sobriety as men well-drunk at a draught of well water. But she, when she had brought her basket with the accustomed festival food, to be but tasted by herself and then given away, never joined therewith more than one small cup of wine, diluted according to her own abstemious habits, which for courtesy she would taste. And if there were many churches of the departed saints to be honored in that manner, she still carried round that same cup; and this, though made watery and unpleasantly heated by carrying about, she would distribute to those about her by small sips; for she sought devotion, not pleasure.[14]

Regrettably, we learn, others were not so abstemious or so well motivated. In Rome, on a Sunday, the drunks were stacked up like cordwood in and around the martyria. Dionysus had become a Christian.

I can think of no nicer way to end our long journey and remind you of the humanity we have sought than to quote one of the epigrams of Ausonius. By and large Ausonius' epigrams are not outstanding—many in fact are just old chestnuts translated from the Greek—but this one is rather special: it is addressed to his wife. It will remind you of Catullus, but he could not help that, and neither can I:

Dearest wife, as we have lived, let us live and hold fast to the names we used when first we met. Let no day alter this for all eternity. I'll always be your boy and you my girl. Though I should outlive Nestor and you Sybillene Deiphobe, we shall never complain of old age. Better to know the worth of time than to count the passage of the years.[15]

And so, to quote Catullus directly, "HAIL AND FAREWELL!"

Chronological Summary

A.D.

303. Diocletian begins last great persecution of Christians.

305. Abdication of Diocletian and Maximian. Galerius and Constantius become emperors.

306. Constantius dies. Constantine the Great acclaimed emperor by his troops.

311. Edict of Toleration by Galerius.

312. Vision of Constantine. Constantine defeats Maxentius, son of Maximian, at Milvian Bridge in Rome.

313. Galerius dies. Constantine and Licinius issue "Edict of Milan."

324. Constantine defeats Licinius and becomes sole emperor.

325. Council of Nicaea.

330. Dedication of New Rome (Constantinople) as capital of the empire.

337. Death of Constantine the Great. Beginning of joint rule of his sons: Constantine II (337-340), Constans (337-350), and Constantius II (337-361).

350. Constantius II sole emperor.

351. Gallus made Caesar.

354. Gallus dies.

355. Julian made Caesar.

360. Julian proclaimed emperor by his troops.
361. Constantius II dies. Julian sole emperor.
363. Persian War. Death of Julian. Jovian made emperor.
364. Jovian dies. Valentinian I and Valens become emperors.
367. Gratian, son of Valentinian, made co-emperor with his father and Valens.
373. Huns appear and attack the Goths in south Russia.
376. Visigoths allowed to cross into Roman territory.
378. Battle of Adrianople. Death of Valens.
379. Theodosius made emperor by Gratian.
382. Altar of Victory removed from the senate house in Rome.
382. Valentinian II made emperor.
383. Gratian dies. Arcadius, son of Theodosius, made emperor.
390. Massacre at Thessalonica. Confrontation of Ambrose and Theodosius.
392. Murder of Valentinian II.
393. Honorius, son of Theodosius, made emperor.
395. Death of Theodosius. Arcadius rules in east and Honorius in the west. Revolt of Alaric and the Visigoths.
396. Alaric driven from Greece by Stilicho the Vandal, general of Arcadius.
405. Vandals invade Italy but are defeated by Stilicho.
408. Stilicho murdered. Arcadius dies. Theodosius II becomes sole emperor in East.
409. Vandals invade Spain.
410. Alaric and his Visigoths capture Rome.
412. Visigoths into Gaul.
415. Visigoths into Spain.
423. Honorius dies. Valentinian III becomes emperor in West.
429. Vandals invade Africa.
430. Death of St. Augustine as Vandals invest Hippo.
438. Promulgation of Theodosian Code.
439. Carthage falls to Vandals.
441. Huns under Attila invade the Balkans.
450. Death of Theodosius II.

Imperial Genealogies

I. CONSTANTIAN DYNASTY

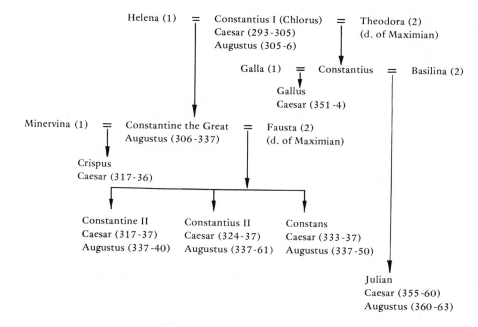

Helena (1) = Constantius I (Chlorus) = Theodora (2)
Caesar (293-305) (d. of Maximian)
Augustus (305-6)

Galla (1) = Constantius = Basilina (2)

Gallus
Caesar (351-4)

Minervina (1) = Constantine the Great = Fausta (2)
Augustus (306-337) (d. of Maximian)

Crispus
Caesar (317-36)

Constantine II
Caesar (317-37)
Augustus (337-40)

Constantius II
Caesar (324-37)
Augustus (337-61)

Constans
Caesar (333-37)
Augustus (337-50)

Julian
Caesar (355-60)
Augustus (360-63)

II. DYNASTY OF VALENTINIAN (AND THEODOSIUS)

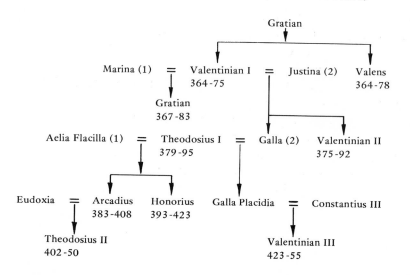

Gratian

Marina (1) = Valentinian I = Justina (2) Valens
364-75 364-78

Gratian
367-83

Aelia Flacilla (1) = Theodosius I = Galla (2) Valentinian II
379-95 375-92

Eudoxia = Arcadius Honorius Galla Placidia = Constantius III
383-408 393-423

Theodosius II
402-50

Valentinian III
423-55

NOTES

Notes

I

1. For interesting biographies of some of these women, see E. Duckett, *Medieval Portraits from East and West*, Ann Arbor 1972.

2. C. Pharr, ed., *The Theodosian Code*, Princeton 1952. Cited henceforth as CT.

3. CT, I, 4. 1.

4. *Ibid.*, II, 10. 3 and 5.

5. *Ibid.*, XIII, 3. 7.

6. *Ibid.*, X, 20. 14.

7. *Ibid.*, VIII, 5. 2.

8. *Ibid.*, VII, 22. 1.

9. Ammianus, XXIX, 1. 25-35.

10. H. P. L'Orange, *Art Forms and Civic Life in the Later Roman Empire*, Princeton 1965.

11. R. Carpenter, "Art in Transition," *The Age of Diocletian* (Metropolitan Museum of Art Symposium on Diocletian), New York 1953, p. 65.

12. Jane Austen, *Northanger Abbey*. For a convenient edition, see Signet Classics, New York, pp. 91-92.

II

1. The text of the Pilgrim of 333 can be found in T. Tobler, *Itinera Hierosolymitana*, Geneva 1879, and there is also a translation in Palestine Pilgrim Text Society publications Vol. I, London 1887; the letter of Paula and Eustochium is no. VI among the letters of St. Jerome; the *Peregrinatio Sanctae Paulae* is included in the Tobler volume cited above; and *Egeria's Travels* has been translated by J. Wilkinson, London 1971.

2. *Peregrinatio*, XVI.

3. Otto Cuntz, *Itineraria Romana*, Leipsic 1929.

133

4. Konrad Miller, *Die Peutingerische Tafel*, Stuttgart 1962. See also, A. C. Levi and B. Trell, "An Ancient Tourist Map," *Archaeology* 17 (1964), pp. 227-36.

5. Ausonius, *The Order of Famous Cities*, XX (trans. by H. G. E. White in the Loeb Classical Library — henceforth LCL — Vol. I, pp. 283-85.

6. *Ibid.*, XVIII, p. 279.

7. *Ibid.*, XIX, p. 281.

8. *Ibid.*, X, p. 277.

9. *Ibid.*, VII, p. 273.

10. *Augustan History*, Aurelian, XXV, 2. 6.

11. Pilgrim of 333, p. 16 (Tobler).

12. *Ibid.*, p. 17.

13. *Ibid.*, p. 18.

14. Wilkinson, *Egeria's Travels*, p. 94.

15. *Ibid.*, p. 103.

16. *Ibid.*, pp. 106-7.

17. *Ibid.*, p. 122.

18. See R. T. Meyer, *Palladius: the Lausiac History*, London 1965, p. 210 where he questions the identity of Silvia as the subject of this passage.

19. *Peregrinatio*, VIII.

20. *Ibid.*, XVIII.

21. *Ibid.*, XIX.

22. Jerome, Letter CXXVII, 8.

23. *Ibid.*, Letter VI.

24. Gregory of Nyssa, "On Pilgrimages," *Select Library of Nicene and Post-Nicene Fathers*, second series V, p. 383 (reprint Grand Rapids 1972).

III

1. *Fontes Iuris Romani Antejustiniani*, II, 544.

2. For inscriptions and monuments of the Sasanian period, see E. Schmidt, *Persepolis*, III, Chicago 1970; E. Herzfeld, "Paikuli," *Forschungen zur islamischen Kunst*, III, Berlin 1924; M. Sprengling, *Third Century Islam*, Chicago 1953; A. Christensen, *L'Iran sous les Sassanids*, Copenhagen 1944; E. Herzfeld, "La sculpture rupestre de la Perse," *Revue des arts asiatiques*, V (1928), pp. 129-42; R. Ghirshman, *Iran*, Harmondsworth 1954; and E. Porada, *The Art of Ancient Iran*, New York, 1965.

3. T. Rice, *Ancient Arts of Central Asia*, New York 1965, p. 197.

4. Ammianus, XIX, 1-8.

5. Eunapius, *Lives of the Philosophers*, 465 (LCL trans. by W. C. Wright, pp. 393-95).

6. Ammianus, XXIII, 6. 75-83.

7. *Ibid.*, XXIV, 6. 1.

IV

1. Libanius, *Oratio I*, 19 (trans. by A. F. Norman, *Libanius, Autobiography*, London 1965, p. 15).

2. *Ibid.*, I, 149.

3. Julian, Letter 9 (trans. by W. C. Wright in LCL, *Julian III*, pp. 27-28).

4. D. Brooke, *Private Letters, Pagan and Christian*, London 1929, CXIII, p. 113.

5. *Ibid.*, CXVI, p. 115.

6. Julian, Letter 23 (in Wright, *Julian III*, p. 73).

7. Libanius, *Oratio I*, 127ff.

8. Gregory Nazianzus, *Against Julian*, II. 30.

9. Prudentius, *Apotheosis*, 1. 454ff.

10. Eutropius, *Breviarium ab urbe condita*, X, 16. For a longer and carefully balanced evaluation of Julian, see Ammianus, XXV, 4. 1-27.

V

1. M. K. L. Clarke, *St. Basil the Great*, Cambridge, Eng. 1913, p. 1, quoting Lecky, *History of European Morals*.

2. *Ibid.*, p. 1, quoting Dean Inge, *Truth and Falsehood in Religion*.

3. Basil, Letter CCXXIII.

4. Clarke, *St. Basil*, p. 23.

5. Gregory Nazianzus, Letter V (trans. in *Select Library of Nicene and Post-Nicene Fathers*, second series, Grand Rapids 1974, Vol. VII, p. 447).

6. R.R.Ruether, *Gregory of Nazianzus, Rhetor and Philosopher*, Oxford, 1969, p. 34.

7. *Ibid.*, pp. 36-37.

8. Gregory Nazianzus, Letter LVIII (trans. in *Select Library*, p. 455.).

9. Basil, Letter CCCIV.

10. D. Brooke, *Private Letters*, CLIII and CLIV, p. 142.

11. *Ibid.*, CLVIII, pp. 144-45.

12. *Ibid.*, CLVII, p. 144.

13. Gregory of Nazianzus, *Epigrams*, no. 158.

14. Gregory of Nyssa, Letter XVI (trans. in *Select Library* V, 1972, p. 540).

15. W. Jaeger, *Early Christianity and Greek Paideia*, Cambridge, Mass. 1961.

16. Ruether, *Gregory*, p. 47.

VI

1. H. I. Bell, *Jews and Christians in Egypt*, Oxford 1924, pp. 61-62.

2. Greek Anthology, IX, 173 (trans. by F. A. Wright, *Poets of the Greek Anthology*, New York 1924, p. 206).

3. *Ibid.*, IX, 171 (Wright, p. 203).

4. *Ibid.*, IX, 175 (Wright, p. 204).

5. *Ibid.*, XI, 378 (trans. Paton, LCL, IV, p. 251).

6. *Ibid.*, X, 381.

7. *Ibid.*, X, 63 (Paton, IV, p. 35).

8. *Ibid.*, IX, 393 (Paton III, p. 219).

9. *Ibid.*, X, 90 (Wright, p. 218).

10. *Ibid.*, XI, 384 (Paton IV, p. 255).

11. *Ibid.*, IX, 489 (Paton, III, p. 273).

12. *Ibid.*, VII, 610 (Paton, II, p. 327).

13. H. I. Bell, *The Abinnaeus Archive*, Oxford 1962.
14. *Ibid.*, Letter 2, p. 38.

VII

1. C. H. Kraeling, *Ptolemais, City of the Libyan Pentapolis*, Chicago 1962.
2. CT, XV, 6. 1.
3. *Ibid.*, XV, 6. 2.
4. Greek Anthology, IX, 400 (trans. Paton, LCL, III, p. 223).
5. *Ibid.*, IX, 202.
6. D. Brooke, *Private Letters*, CLII, pp. 141-42.
7. Greek Anthology, III, 202.
8. Socrates, *Ecclesiastical History*, VII, 5.
9. A. Fitzgerald, *Letters of Synesius of Cyrene*, Oxford 1926, Letter 54, pp. 125-26.
10. *Ibid.*, Letter 136, p. 229.
11. *Ibid.*, Letter 104, p. 91.
12. *Ibid.*, Letter 105, p. 199.
13. *Ibid.*, Letter 132, p. 224.
14. *Ibid.*, Letter 108, p. 203.
15. *Ibid.*, Letter 104, pp. 195-96.
16. *Ibid.*, Letter 110, p. 110.
17. *Ibid.*, Letter 58, pp. 142-43.
18. *Ibid.*, Letter 16, pp. 99-100.

VIII

1. Ammianus, XVI, 10. 9-17.
2. Jerome, *Commentary on Ezekiel*, XII, 40. 468.
3. Ammianus, XXVIII, 4. 14.
4. *Ibid.*, XIV, 6. 12.
5. *Ibid.*, XXVIII, 4. 29-52.
6. *Ibid.*, XIV, 6. 19.
7. *Ibid.*, XXVII. 3, 12-13.
8. H. P. V. Nunn, *Christian Inscriptions*, New York 1951, p. 49.
9. Jerome, Letter XXII, 16.
10. *Ibid.*, Letter XXII, 27-28.
11. J. A. McGeachy, *Q. Aurelius Symmachus*, Chicago 1942, p. 8.
12. Ausonius, *Epistles* (trans. White, LCL, II, pp. 2-7).
13. Symmachus, *Relatio de ara Victoriae*, 3. 10.
14. Augustine, *Confessions*, VI, 2.
15. Ausonius, *Epigrams*, no. 40.

SELECT BIBLIOGRAPHY

Select Bibliography

Arnheim, M. T. W. *The Senatorial Aristocracy in the Later Roman Empire*. Oxford: Clarendon, 1972.

Barrow, R. H. *Prefect and Emperor: the* Relationes *of Symmachus, A.D. 384*. Oxford, Clarendon, 1973.

Bell, H. I. *The Abinnaeus Archive*. Oxford: Clarendon, 1962.

Bidez, J. *La vie de l'empereur Julien*. Paris: Les Belles Lettres, 1930.

Binns, J. W., ed. *Latin Literature of the Fourth Century*. London: Routledge Kegan Paul, 1974.

Brooke, D. *Pilgrims Were They All*. London: Faber, 1937.

Brown, P. R. L. *Augustine of Hippo*. Berkeley: University of California Press, 1967.

————. *The World of Late Antiquity*. London: Thames & Hudson, 1971.

Browning, R. *The Emperor Julian*. Berkeley: University of California Press, 1976.

Bury, J. B. *The Late Roman Empire*, 2 vols. New York: Dover, 1958.

Cameron, A. D. E. "The Roman Friends of Ammianus," *Journal of Roman Studies*, 54 (1964), pp. 15-28.

Christensen, A. *L'Iran sous les Sassanids*, 2nd ed. Copenhagen: Munksgaard, 1944.

Cochrane, C. M. *Christianity and Classical Culture*. New York: Galaxy, 1960.

Cramer, F. H. *Astrology in Roman Law and Politics*. Philadelphia: American Philosophical Society, 1954.

Davies, P. V., tr. *Macrobius, The Saturnalia*. New York: Columbia University Press, 1969.

Dill, S. *Roman Society in the Last Century of the Western Empire*. New York, Meridian, 1958.

Downey, G. *Ancient Antioch*. Princeton: Princeton University Press, 1962.

————. *Antioch in the Age of Theodosius the Great*. Norman, Okla.: University of Oklahoma Press, 1962.

————. *The Late Roman Empire*. New York: Holt, Rinehart & Winston, 1969.

Duckett, E. *Medieval Portraits from East and West*. Ann Arbor: University of Michigan Press, 1972.

Dudden, F. H. *The Life and Times of St. Ambrose*, 2 vols. Oxford: Oxford University Press, 1935.

Festugière, A. M. J. *Antioche païenne et chrétienne*. Paris: Boccard, 1959.

Fitzgerald, A. *The Letters of Synesius of Cyrene*. Oxford: Oxford University Press, 1926.

Frye, R. N. *The Heritage of Persia*. Cleveland: World, 1963.

Ghirshman, R. *Ancient Iran*. Harmondsworth, Eng.: Penguin, 1956.

Gibbon, E. (edited by J. B. Bury). *The Decline and Fall of the Roman Empire*, 7 vols. London: Methuen, 1897-1902.

Glover, T. R. *Life and Letters in the Fourth Century*. Cambridge: Cambridge University Press, 1901.

Goffart, W. *Caput and Colonate; Toward a History of Late Roman Taxation*. Toronto: University of Toronto Press, 1973.

Hunt, E. D. "St. Silvia of Aquitaine," *Journal of Theological Studies*, n.s., XXIII (1972), pp. 317-73.

Jaeger, W. *Early Christianity and Greek Paideia*. Cambridge: Harvard University Press, 1961.

Jones, A. H. M. *The Later Roman Empire*, 2 vols. Norman, Okla.: University of Oklahoma Press, 1964.

Kaegi, W. *Byzantium and the Decline of Rome*. Princeton: Princeton University Press, 1968.

Katz, S. *The Decline of Rome and the Rise of Medieval Europe*. Ithaca: Cornell University Press, 1955.

Kraeling, C. H. *Ptolemais, City of the Libyan Pentapolis*. Chicago: University of Chicago Press, 1962.

Laistner, M. L. W. *The Conflict between Pagans and Christians in the Fourth Century*. Oxford: Clarendon, 1963.

———. *Christianity and Pagan Culture in the Later Roman Empire*. Ithaca: Cornell University Press, 1967.

Levi, D. *Antioch Mosaic Pavements*. Princeton: Princeton University Press, 1947.

Liebeschutz, J. H. W. G. *Antioch, City and Imperial Administration in the Later Roman Empire*. Oxford: Clarendon, 1972.

L'Orange, H. P. *Art Forms and Civic Life in the Later Roman Empire*. Princeton: Princeton University Press, 1965.

MacMullen, R. *Soldier and Civilian in the Later Roman Empire*. Cambridge: Harvard University Press, 1963.

Matthews, J. F. *Western Aristocracies and the Imperial Court, A.D. 364-425*. Oxford: Clarendon, 1975.

McGeachy, J. A. *Q. Aurelius Symmachus and the Senatorial Aristocracy of the West*. Chicago: Dissertation, 1942.

Millar, F., ed. *The Roman Empire and Its Neighbors*. New York: Delacorte, 1967.

Momigliano, A., ed. *The Conflict between Paganism and Christianity in the Fourth Century*, Oxford: Oxford University Press, 1963.

Morrison, K. F. *Rome and the City of God*. Philadelphia: American Philosophical Society, 1964.

Norman, A. F. *Libanius, Autobiography* (Oratio I). London: Oxford University Press, 1965.

Oost, S. I. *Galla Placidia Augusta*. Chicago: Chicago University Press, 1968.

Petit, P. *Libanius et la vie municipale à Antioch*. Paris: Guethner, 1955.

———. *Les étudiants de Libanius*. Paris: Nouvelles Ed. Lat., 1957.

Pharr, C., ed. *The Theodosian Code*. Princeton: Princeton University Press, 1952.

Porada, E. *The Art of Ancient Iran*. New York: Crown, 1965.

Ruether, R. R. *Gregory of Nazianzus, Rhetor and Philosopher*, Oxford, Clarendon, 1969.

Rowell, H. *Ammianus Marcellinus, Soldier-Historian of the Late Roman Empire*. Cincinnati: University of Cincinnati Press, 1964.

Sambursky, S. *Physical World of Late Antiquity*. New York: Basic Books, 1962.

Setton, K. *Christian Attitudes towards the Emperor in the Fourth Century*. New York: Columbia University Press, 1941.

Starr, C. G. *Civilization and the Caesars*. New York: Norton, 1965.

Syme, R. *Ammianus and the Historia Augusta*. Oxford: Clarendon, 1968.

Thompson, E. A. *The Historical Work of Ammianus Marcellinus*. Cambridge: Cambridge University Press, 1947.

———. *A Roman Reformer and Inventor*. Oxford: Oxford University Press, 1952.

Vogt, J. *The Decline of Rome*. New York: New American Library, 1967.

Walden, J. H. W. *The Universities of Ancient Greece*. New York: Scribners, 1909.

Wilkinson, J. *Egeria's Travels*. London: Society for the Promotion of Christian Knowledge, 1971.

INDEX

Index

Abinnaeus, Flavius (soldier), 89-95
Adrianople, Battle of, 5, 7, 55
Alaric, 5, 106
Alexandria in Egypt, 83, 99-101
Altar of Victory, 122, 124
Ambrose, St. (Bishop of Milan), 111, 122-24
Ammianus Marcellinus (historian), 7, 11, 50, 96, 111, 112, 113-15
Antioch in Syria, 52-56
Architecture, 15, 54, 79-80
Ardashir I (Sasanian king), 39
Art, 15-16, 51, 53-54, 111-112
Astrology, 11, 60, 62, 97, 106, 111, 115
Athanasius (Bishop of Alexandria), 83-84
Athens, schools of, 58-59, 100, 103-4
Augustine, St. (Bishop of Hippo), 5, 7, 111, 125-27
Ausonius (poet), 26-28, 111, 121-22, 127

Barbarians, 3, 5, 37, 107
Basil, St. (Bishop of Caesarea), 5, 69-81, 101-2
Bethlehem, 35, 118
Bordeaux pilgrim, 21, 24-31

Cappadocian Trinity (Basil, Gregory of Nyssa, Gregory Nazianzus), 69ff.
Chrysostom, St. John, 53, 56, 106-7
Church and state, 4
Claque, theatrical: at Antioch, 55; at Rome, 115
Claudian (poet), 85, 111
Constantine the Great (Roman emperor), 3, 4, 8, 9, 30
Constantius II (Roman emperor), 48, 61-62, 92

Damasus, Pope, 115-17
Daphne, festival of Apollo at, 66
Dead Sea, 30
Diocletian (Roman emperor), 3, 91, 99

Education of children, 86
Egeria, pilgrimage of, 21, 31-33
Egypt, organization of, 83
Epigrams, of Gregory Nazianzus, 79, 85; of Palladas, 84-89, 101
Eustathius (sophist), 49, 64
Eutropius (historian), 68

Gainas (general), 5, 107
Galla Placidia, 5
Golden House of Constantine, 54, 79

Greek Anthology, 85
Gregory Nazianzus, St., 67, 69, 73-81, 126
Gregory, St., of Nyssa, 35, 69, 72-73, 79-80
Guilds, 10

Helena, St., 5, 22
Historical interpretation, 17
Hypatia (philosopher and scientist), 5, 100-103, 110

Ignatius, Bishop, 53
Inscriptions, sepulchral, 12-14
Itineraries, 24-25

Jericho, 30
Jerome, St., 4, 7, 21-22, 111, 113, 115ff.
Jerusalem, 30
Julian the Apostate (Roman emperor), 6, 8, 56, 58, 60, 61-68, 74, 80, 85

Lawyers and jurists, 9, 97, 115
Libanius, 53, 56-61, 66-68, 96

Macrina, St. (sister of St. Basil), 71, 74, 80
Majuma, 99
Manichaeans, 42-44
Maximus of Ephesus (sophist), 61-62
Meletians, 83-84
Monasticism, 4-5, 70-72, 75, 88

Olympic games at Antioch, 54
Orthodoxy, 4

Palladas (poet), 84-89, 101
Papyri, 90-91
Paula, pilgrimage of, 21, 33-35, 117-18
Peutinger Table, 24-25
Pilgrimage, 20ff.
Prudentius (poet), 67, 120
Ptolemais in Cyrene, 98-99
Ptolemy, Claudius (scientist), 100

Riot of the Statues, 55-56
Rome, city of, 111-15, 118-19

Sasanians, 38ff.
Shapur I (Sasanian king), 39-40
Shapur II (Sasanian king), 40, 44-56, 82
Slavery, 10
Stilicho (general), 5, 107
Symmachus, Quintus Aurelius, 57, 111, 120, 122-24
Synesius (Bishop of Cyrene), 96ff.

Theodosian Code, 7-11, 18, 97, 99
Theodosius the Great (Roman emperor), 6, 12, 124
Theodosius II (Roman emperor), 3, 5, 7
Theon (scientist, father of Hypatia), 100-101
Tomb robbing, 11, 12, 79

Valens (Roman emperor), 5, 12, 60, 70, 72, 76

Zoroastrianism, 42-44, 47-48